KITCHENS

Design Is in the Details

KITCHENS

Design Is in the Details

Brad Mee

Sterling Publishing Co., Inc. New York
A Sterling/Chapelle Book

Chapelle, Limited

Owner: Jo Packham

Editor: Karmen Potts Quinney

Editorial Assistant: Susan Jorgensen

Cover Image: Wood-Mode

If you have any questions or comments, please contact:
Chapelle, Ltd., Inc., P.O. Box 9252 Ogden, UT 84409
(801) 621-2777 • FAX (801) 621-2788
• e-mail: chapelle@chapelleltd.com
• website: www.chapelleltd.com

Library of Congress Cataloging-in-Publication Data Available

10 9 8 7 6 5 4 3 2 1

Published by Sterling Publishing Co., Inc.,
387 Park Avenue South, New York, NY 10016
© 2002 by Brad Mee
Distributed in Canada by Sterling Publishing
⅝ Canadian Manda Group, One Atlantic Avenue, Suite 105
Toronto, Ontario, Canada M6K 3E7
Distributed in Great Britain and Europe by Cassell PLC
Wellington House, 125 Strand, London WC2R 0BB, England
Distributed in Australia by Capricorn Link (Australia) Pty. Ltd.
P.O. Box 704, Windsor, NSW 2756, Australia
Printed in China
All Rights Reserved

Sterling ISBN 0-8069-8569-0

Introduction 8

CONTENTS

RECIPES OF STYLE 10

Comforting Style 12

Inspired Style 18

Disciplined Style 24

Imported Style 30

Artistic Style 36

PRESENTATION 42

Underfoot 44

Verticals 50

Overhead 56

Cabinets 62

BASIC INGREDIENTS	68	SPICE	90	PERFORMANCE	116
Appliances	70	Accessories	92	Cook-in	118
Countertops	76	Display	98	Dine-in	122
Lighting	82	Hanging On	102	Live-in	128
		Working Accents	108	Off the Kitchen	134
		Color	110	Acknowledgments	141
				Credits	142
				Index	144

INTRODUCTION

Not so long ago, the kitchen was simply defined as the room created to facilitate cooking. Today, this utilitarian definition hardly touches on the dynamic personality of this bustling space. These days, the kitchen is the heart of the home. In fact, the average household spends more of its time in the kitchen than in any other room. It has far outgrown its straightforward cooking role, and in many cases, serves as the family room, dining room, home office, and social center of everyday living. It is no wonder that the design and character of the "multitalented" kitchen has become so important to the home's inhabitants.

The kitchen, like any other room in which one spends a great deal of time, deserves the character and style that creative detail brings to a space. *Kitchens: Design Is in the Details* explores this avenue. This book is not a technical guide to kitchen planning, but is, instead, a celebration of the many elements of design that, when combined, give a kitchen its own spirit. Today, the decorative detail that was once reserved for other rooms now flourishes in the home's kitchen. Colors, textures, objects, and imaginative treatments fill the space, taking their cue from the attentive design and decoration once saved for lavish living rooms, stunning dining rooms and even the well-appointed professional kitchens of fine restaurants.

Clearly, the kitchen performs differently for different people. To some, it acts as the communal core of the home and is created with this social aspect in mind.

Others use it solely as a creative center for cooking and prize it as a studio for culinary adventures. Still others make it an extension of the vivacious living area of the home. However your kitchen performs for you, detail can be used to both enrich the activities and enhance the atmosphere of your space.

When you see a kitchen that excites and embraces you, you will find detail everywhere. Some may be alive with overwhelming decoration while the impact of others is created by restrained, yet creative, touches of personal style. Surfaces may gleam under brilliant tile, warm wood, or sleek stainless steel. Painted murals, unique finishes, or richly patterned papers may dress the space. Appliances may be camouflaged with distinctive treatments or highlighted with stunning fixtures. Cabinetry and furniture may be paired like perfectly teamed partners, dancing beneath carefully selected lighting, adding to the room's ambience. Accessories and accents flourish throughout, becoming the finishing touches that punctuate the owner's personal style. This is the magic that detail can bring to a kitchen —the magic that you will find illustrated in this book.

Explore the following pages and study the many imaginative uses of detail found within. Glean the ideas that inspire you. Shape them with your own unique style and lavish them upon your own kitchen. The result will be a working, spirited room that reflects your own definition of the kitchen—a space alive with character and personality that is distinctively yours.

If you have an appetite for style, your kitchen is the perfect place to bring personality and character into your home. And, as in a favorite recipe, mixing a number of flavorful ingredients can result in a unique creation that reflects your individual taste. Details are the all-important ingredients that take an ordinary unadorned room and turn it into a personal statement of style. They can give a characterless kitchen the look of a quaint cottage or, just as easily, a sophisticated modern loft. All the recipe requires is direction. With your likes and individual style as a guide, you can use detail to create a look that suits your taste perfectly.

What is your design preference? What way do you bend intuitively? Do you prefer the relaxed feel of a country kitchen or the clarity of a sleek, contemporary one? These and other specific styles have basic ingredients that can be used to create a desired look. Elegantly styled kitchens, for instance, often share common design elements. By contrast, so do understated modern kitchens. By recognizing some of these basic "recipes" you can use them to help create your own special concoction. Consider your favorites from these tasty details and incorporate them with your own style to create the kitchen of your dreams.

Inviting, soothing, nurturing, . . . these three words describe one of the most popular design directions for the kitchen—the comforting kitchen. Life is lived in this room. Here, pets are fed, homework is completed, cakes are frosted, and casual dinners are enjoyed with family and friends. Cooking is an integral part of this room as it supports the social role of the room. In design, comforting does not mean folksy; it means warm and welcoming. This kitchen can be lavishly or simply decorated as long as it is alive with earthy details that enhance its soulful vitality. Here, nature is valued above all. Everyday cookware and utensils are proudly displayed and used. Modern gadgets like electric juicers and food processors are hidden from view because they intrude on the natural sense of the space. Herbs grow on the windowsills and everyday dishes are displayed on open shelves or behind glass-front cabinet

COMFORTING STYLE

doors. Collected glass storage jars sit empty or hold dried pasta, preserved fruit, or handpicked wildflowers as they perch on top of tile or butcher-block countertops. Ropes of garlic or chilies decorate the walls, as do baskets, framed art, or bulletin boards covered with notes and family pictures. Sunlight is cherished and windows are left unadorned or dressed casually with patterned cotton or linen fabrics. Brick, tile, or wooden floors offer practicality and complement distressed or freshly painted cabinetry decorated with unpretentious hardware. There are many faces of the comforting kitchen. Country French, Tuscan, Shaker, and Arts & Crafts are all varieties of this style. So are Scandinavian and American Country designs. In all of these, inviting detail that speaks of a natural uncomplicated life and that offers contentment and uncontrived beauty is perfectly at home. For this is a kitchen that is proud to look and act as a kitchen. It is an inspirational room that embraces all who enter with warmth and charm.

The pleasure of a comforting kitchen is derived from its simple natural approach to detail. It has a relaxed tenor reflecting the owners' desire to surround themselves with a familiar setting that slows the pulse and warms the heart. The key to decorating a comforting kitchen is keeping it casual and unpretentious. Formality is out. So is stylized and symmetric display. Here, favored objects are effortlessly displayed and placed rather than staged throughout the room. Many of the room's accessories are everyday tools of the kitchen—stoneware, wooden spatulas, crockery, dried herbs, and cotton dish towels. Treasured antiques and yard-sale finds are at home here. An old hutch, grandmother's mismatched china, and sisal rugs speak of simplicity, while warm mellowed finishes and harmonious colors enhance the wood, tile, and hand-painted surfaces throughout. The room's working necessities are partnered with timeworn collectibles and personal mementos. Copper pots and wicker baskets pair perfectly with family photos and favorite cookbooks on shelves and in open cupboards. Keeping the detail simple, natural, and meaningful makes a welcoming statement of comfort and personal style.

PAGE 13
Unfitted cabinets and mismatched heirloom finishes contribute to the uncontrived nature of this Country French kitchen. Beautifully carved woodwork, yellow-ochre glazed pottery, and hand-forged hardware speak the flavor of earthy Provence.

LEFT AND OPPOSITE
Sophisticated, yet comfortable, this kitchen derives its personality from the strength and simplicity of the Craftsman style. The embracing design employs freshly finished cabinetry perfectly teamed with bold architecture, glowing wooden floors, and wonderfully colored tile and fabrics.

PAGE 16
Honoring the purity of the Shaker style, this kitchen derives its vitality from abundant authentic decorative touches. Colorful oval boxes, orderly plate racks, rustic beams, and boxy aged-looking cabinetry reflect the uncluttered integrity of the Shaker look. Modern appliances are hidden or downplayed to avoid distraction from the homespun theme.

COMFORTING INGREDIENTS

butcher-block countertops
hand-formed tile
woven-rush seats
waffle-weave dish towels
screen doors
grape-stake wreaths
freshly cut flowers

open display shelves
dried herbs
copper molds
hardwood floors
terra-cotta
rustic baskets
mason jars

hanging pot rack
cast-iron cookware
spice racks
flea-market glassware
porcelain drawer pulls
distressed finishes
rough-hewn beams

framed botanical prints
wire-mesh cabinet doors
weathered wicker
hand-dipped candles
painted furniture
skirted sinks
patterned table linens

Guests of the inspired kitchen are treated to a highly stylized, somewhat traditional and absolutely non-kitcheny space. In the inspired kitchen, atmosphere is everything. The room performs well as a kitchen, yet it feels more like an elegant entertaining or dining room. Detail is used to mask the functional purpose of the kitchen and to highlight its refined, sophisticated side. So that the room appears furnished rather than equipped, appliances are disguised to look like the finely crafted cabinetry that surrounds them. Freestanding furniture is also incorporated in the space—an armoire here, an antique desk there. In this room, cooking is an art and is executed in richly stimulating surroundings. Elegant granite and marble countertops shine under recessed lights, a chandelier, or even shaded lamps. Glossy cookbooks, professional cutlery, and a built-in wine rack speak of the fine dining enjoyed in the room. Ornately framed art, antique rugs, and faux-finished walls

INSPIRED STYLE

reinforce the un-kitchen-like feel of the room. The cook's tools are of the finest quality, but are discretely hidden until the culinary enthusiast needs them. Only sparkling glassware, cherished dinnerware, and silver are typically displayed. Visually and intellectually stirring, this room is adorned with detail that lends an elegant orderly air to the sanctuary known as the inspired kitchen.

Living well is the best revenge.

George Herbert

It may require a double take to recognize the inspired kitchen as the home's "cooking" room. Here, you are as likely to see a chandelier, elaborate crown moldings, and elegantly framed art as you are to see a refrigerator or oven. In fact, the latter may be hard to find behind their beautifully carved wooden door panels. In this kitchen, detail plays off the artistic and seductive nature of food, as decorative elements, once saved for the more polished areas of the home, are incorporated to create a refined elegant ambience in which to cook and dine.

PAGE 19
An arresting collection of copper coffee pots adds immeasurably to the elegance of this beautifully refined kitchen. Honed granite, coliseum stone floors, and richly finished wood, once saved for grand living rooms, are at home in this enlightened setting.

OPPOSITE AND RIGHT
As viewed through an open arch or from across the room, this kitchen offers a profusion of details that speak of cultured elegant living. An enormous boldly carved cabinet lords over antique rugs, stone floors, granite countertops and an assortment of fine dishware staged behind sparkling glass-front cabinet doors.

PAGE 23
When part of an open floor plan, the kitchen needs to incorporate detail of neighboring spaces to support the overall style of the interior. This kitchen's exquisitely carved cabinets, stunning surface treatments, and eclectic accessories mirror those of the home's richly appointed living and dining areas.

INSPIRED INGREDIENTS

wine racks
faux-finished walls
glossy cookbooks
granite countertops
richly carved armoires
unfitted cabinetry
bone china

candelabra
luxurious draperies
still-life oil painting
topiaried ivy
dimmer switches
monogrammed flatware
crystal decanters

shaded table lamps
polished hardware
copper crepe pan
trompe l'oeil
gilded mirrors
imported tile
complete silver service

fondue pot
flatware chest
marble mortar & pestle
espresso machine
upholstered seating
richly-woven tapestries
beeswax candles

"Less is more" describes the decorative approach taken in a disciplined kitchen. Here, everything has a purpose and nothing is superfluous. Design is employed, but aesthetics are balanced with practicality. To some, this look is cold and sparse, while to others, it is a paradise free of clutter and inefficiency. On the surface, it may appear that detail plays a small role in the design of this kitchen; but, in fact, the disciplined kitchen is as artfully created as any other style. Here, detail takes shape in the execution of the design elements rather than in their abundance. Its presence creates a unique sense of style and personality—no matter how understated. For the lover of the disciplined kitchen, clarity of mind is achieved through organization and neatness. Detail comes alive in the

DISCIPLINED STYLE

intriguing interplay of fixtures, materials, and finishes. Streamlined cabinetry is uniformly shaped and accented with concealed or inconspicuous hardware. Granite or stainless-steel countertops perform for the orderly chef, while professional appliances and efficient lighting aid in the culinary endeavors. Floors may be concrete, stone, or even lightly finished wood; but this is no place for patterned tile or ornate rugs. Frosted- or etched-glass cabinet fronts divulge a mysterious hint of what they hold inside. Halogen lighting is suspended by wires or unobtrusively mounted in the ceiling and cabinets. To create a harmonized ambience that is simple but not sterile, solid planes of color, clean lines, and luminous finishes are used. Detail is not only evident in what you do see, but also in what you do not. There are no decorative moldings or cornices adding unnecessary drama. Fabric window coverings are verboten—blinds, louvers, or shudders provide the needed privacy. When kitchens of this nature are well executed, they are proof that a systematic organized room can be as dramatic and stylish as the most ornately decorated spaces.

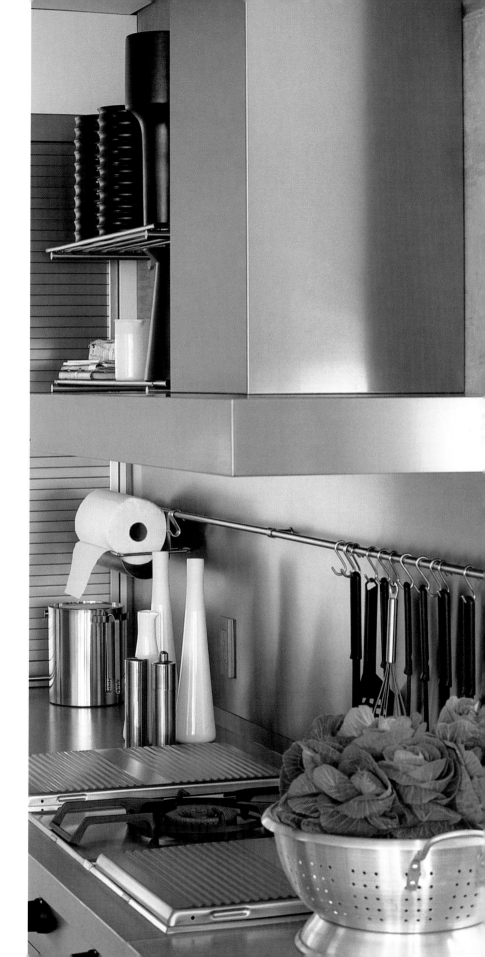

A house is a machine for living in.

Le Corbusier

The idea that a disciplined kitchen is created with endless planes of polished metal and high-tech fixtures is a thing of the past. Today's version boasts an intriguing, almost sensual feel resulting from the shapes of its fixtures, the luminosity of its surfaces, and the power of its lighting. Polished stone, gleaming wood, and waxed concrete enhance the space without jeopardizing its practical nature. Backsplashes of glass tile, stone, or metal perform well here, as do frosted-glass door fronts and stainless-steel sinks. The tools of the kitchen— cookware, utensils and dinnerware—are chosen based on their quality and functional value. Here, when a choice is necessary, understated clean lines win over stylized design every time.

PAGE 25
A gleaming curved hood is juxtaposed with square-angled cabinetry to create clean, intriguing lines. Color and surface materials—steel, wood, and granite—have been brilliantly exploited to dramatically enhance this kitchen's appearance.

OPPOSITE
By combining the ingredients of a professional kitchen—open shelves, fitted lower cabinets, stainless-steel appliances, and unadorned windows—with the warmth of pale woods, dramatic lighting, and hazy glass-front doors, this kitchen becomes an efficient, yet comfortable room for the cooking enthusiast.

RIGHT
Placed close at hand, smartly designed kitchen utensils and canisters are arranged to serve both as display and functional cooking tools.

PAGE 29
The interplay of intriguing materials and finishes gives this functional kitchen an innovative textural-rich look. A cast-in-place concrete and stainless-steel wall treatment, new-age laminate cabinets, synthetic concrete countertops, and white oak floors, all contribute to the room's stylistic strength.

DISCIPLINED INGREDIENTS

glass block
halogen lighting
austere hardware
polished chrome
open skylights
bistro glassware

industrial building materials
translucent cabinet fronts
high-tech design
forged German cutlery
granite slabs
professional appliances

open shelves
recessed lighting
free-form furniture
high-gloss wooden floors
streamlined cabinetry
Roman blinds

luminous finishes
concrete work surfaces
bold color statements
brushed stainless steel
calibrated measuring spoons
plain white dinnerware

Some detail is strongly associated with the look and feel of a specific place or location. When the details of a place are used to enhance the kitchen, they can almost transport you there. Seashells, cotton duck, and bleached wood speak of life at the beach. Saltillo tile, potted cacti, and rich earthy tones reflect the flavor of the Southwest. Many individuals use the flavor of their home's geographical location to determine the decoration of the kitchen. Others use the character of a loved, faraway land to guide the room's design direction. In either case, detail takes shape in the materials, forms, colors, and styles that are indigenous to the chosen land. At every turn, detail awakens an association with a strongly distinctive setting. The kitchen of a

IMPORTED STYLE

mountain cabin is a natural for rough-hewn beams, antler chandeliers, rustic pottery, and richly woven Native American rugs. Legless chairs and a low table resting on tatami mats complement the lacquered pottery and tranquil lighting of a Japanese-styled kitchen. The key is determining the distinctive style that inspires and charms you. It is wise, however, to evaluate the actual setting of the home. While introducing the detail of another place can be comfortable and fitting even when it is taken out of its original context, there are times when it may feel unsuitable and incompatible with its new setting. You be the judge. If the detail feels right, is not obtrusive and, most of all makes you happy, your kitchen may be the perfect place to import the distinctive flavor of your favorite place.

> *We shape our dwellings. And afterwards*
> *our dwellings shape us.*
>
> Winston Churchill

Can a kitchen decorated as an Italian bistro persuade you to linger at the table a little longer? Does a Japanese-style space promote a moment of serenity and tranquility? In many cases, the imported kitchen reflects more than a preferred decorative style; it implies a desired way of life. Capturing the power of association, detail can communicate both the look and style of living in faraway lands. The influence of the favored locale asserts itself by touching all the senses. Visually, color, pattern, and form are strongly related to specific cultures and locations. The brilliant hues of the Caribbean and the animal prints of the Serengeti imply their regional style. The touch of rough stone or unfinished woodwork may speak of rugged mountain sides, while sleek and simple surfaces depict refreshing Scandinavian simplicity. Aroma, too, can transport a kitchen as scented potpourri and spiced candles conjure up images of distinct locations. Oftentimes, the most common of kitchen necessities—table linens, silverware, and dishware—are used to impact the kitchen with the look and feel of another place. Even the simplest detail, a French café carafe or African wooden jug, can be the initial element that begins the journey of your imported kitchen.

PAGE 34
No detail is left untouched in this charming lodge-look kitchen. Plaids, knotty pine walls, collected copper, and a kitchen stove framed with rocks from a nearby stream all contribute to the character of this mountain home.

OPPOSITE
Bright fiesta colors, worm wood cabinetry, equipole (pig skin) furniture, and thick saltillo tile establish the look and feel of a fun-filled Mexican cantina.

RIGHT
The rustic feel of the desert Southwest is captured in this room's accents. Steer-hide chairs, chiseled countertop edges, saguaro-spine door fronts, and richly carved cabinetry create the room's distinctive look.

IMPORTED INGREDIENTS

indigenous materials
hand-forged hardware
decorative ceramics
ethnic prints
architectural finds

hand-painted tile
foreign cookbooks
organic shapes
imported rugs

unexpected furnishings
scented candles
cherished souvenirs
patterned woven blankets

fabric wall hangings
lacquered boxes
native artifacts
vivid & spicy colors
travel mementos

Created with the same passion and creative fervor as a Picasso canvas, the kitchen is, in many homes, an artistic expression of its owners. This style of kitchen perfunctorily performs its domestic duties. However, its true virtue is the pleasure and admiration derived from its distinctively combined forms, textures, and colors.

ARTISTIC STYLE

It celebrates the owner's individuality while giving a shoulder-shrugging irreverence about what is practical, proper, or expected. When there is a question, form wins over function every time. Architectural elements are exaggerated and raw and unusual materials are exploited throughout. Dramatic lighting is extremely important and imaginative fixtures are employed. Furniture becomes sculpture. Intriguing accessories and accents invite closer inspection for understanding and possible appreciation. This is not a kitchen designed to comfort, but to excite. The artistic kitchen is truly a reflection of the creator's personality. To the owner of this space, art is not considered a luxury, it is a necessity.

Color, form, texture, and tone are all elements creatively incorporated into any work of art. They are also the essence of the detail found in an artistic kitchen. This space places inspiration before institution, as the kitchen, in its originality, is an honest reflection of its owner's personal style. As with sculpture, no material—natural or industrial—is off-limits. Lighting is used as much as an accent itself as a way to brighten other elements in the room. Color, and a play of light and shadows, heighten the dramatic impact of bold architecture. Distinctive accessories and furnishings that are uncommon to a kitchen bring a strong statement of style through the inclusion of their unique forms. Even common utensils and everyday dishes are judged more by their stylistic strength than their functional value. As each passionately chosen element is included in this unusual kitchen, the room's one-of-a-kind look comes alive.

PAGE 36
A sinuous track of lights punctuates the curves and corners of this surface-rich space. Color is spare, used to intrigue but not overwhelm.

OPPOSITE
The spectacle of this kitchen is, in part, created by its lack of walls. Instead, dramatic lighting, a sculptured ceiling, and contoured, fitted cabinetry defines its unique space.

LEFT
From the sandblasted-glass backsplash to the open overhead cubes, artistic details are used to repeat the geometric genius of this strikingly architectural kitchen.

ABOVE
So that the room doesn't look like a mishmash of dynamic treatments, an artistic kitchen requires strong statements of color or materials to "hold" the room together. Here, this is accomplished with a brilliant tile backsplash and the repeated use of burnished stainless steel throughout the confined space.

PAGE 40
In artistic spaces, bold architecture demands strong intriguing surfaces. Concrete, corrugated stainless steel, black granite, and wood combine to define the style of this kitchen. Free-form stools and glass accessories add to the genius of the design.

ARTISTIC INGREDIENTS

dynamic colors
reflective finishes
hand-tooled flatware
suspended mobiles

textured surfaces
colored luminaries
geometric patterns
sleek hardware

glass & art tiles
raw construction materials
ingenious architecture
sculptured accessories

asymmetric arrangements
distinctive light fixtures
avante-garde furniture
exposed duct work

The structural components of the kitchen—the floors, walls, and ceilings—create the backdrop for everything else in the room. They set the tone for the style of the space as color, texture, and pattern adorn their surfaces. Adjust or remove the character of any one of these architectural elements, and the atmosphere of the kitchen changes dramatically. Its ambience becomes altered. Sure, you can take away an appliance, piece of furniture, or accessory from the room; but the stylistic effect would be nothing compared to changing the hue of the walls, the figures on the floor, or the creative treatment of the ceiling. This is the power that detail bestows upon these structural parts of the kitchen. Add to these the cabinets that also help frame a kitchen's space, and you have the four major elements that set the stage for the room's other decorative elements. The more detail given to these surfaces—Venetian plaster on the walls, for instance, or rajah slate on the floors—the more attractive the furnishings, accents, and accessories set on them will appear.

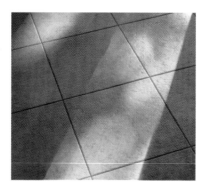

The treatment of surfaces in kitchens requires considerations different from those of other rooms in the home. After all, the kitchen is foremost a practical room with functional needs related to preparing, cooking, and serving food. Beyond its aesthetic appeal, detail must be selected with a consideration of the kitchen's task-oriented nature. It must be able to stand up to both the functional and decorative requirements of the space. Simply put, "if it can't take the heat in the kitchen," (as well as the traffic, messes, and abuse) . . . well, you know how it goes.

Imagine living the life of a kitchen floor. Every day you would be expected to look beautiful while standing up to the endless ordeals this room promises. The dog tracking mud and grass, the kids slopping slush from their galoshes and the in-house cooks and kitchen marauders spilling and dropping every imaginable concoction on your surface. Oh, don't forget about the endless scrapes, scratches, and stains that threaten your appearance. All this and you are

UNDERFOOT

still supposed to be both beautiful and comfortable underfoot. Now, that's not an easy life. With this picture in mind, it becomes clear that practicality is a critical consideration when choosing the way to dress the kitchen floor. There are a number of options, each with features that are functionally beneficial. At the same time, they offer the opportunity to be used independently or together, becoming the "foundation" for a distinctive detailed kitchen.

Even the simplest of flooring materials can be infused with detail to enrich the design of the kitchen. Consider the impact of color. It sets the mood of the room while, when properly chosen, disguising dirt and grime. Pattern can also accomplish this. The stylized placement and patterns of ceramic tile, wood, and stone can be dynamic in the movement it lends to a room. The sheen of a material adds to the ambience of the space. However, remember that a high gloss can act as a mirror, making specks of dirt and pet hair more obvious. And who says only one material can be used? Consider combining materials to bring a unique look to your kitchen's floor—wood inlaid with colorful tiles, vinyl beneath treasured area rugs, and stone accented with marble insets. These are just a few of the endless possibilities. A word of advise: keep in mind the other surfaces you plan for the room when you are selecting the flooring material. These design elements should complement each other either through contrast or similarity. Additionally, take note of floors in adjoining rooms and ponder the idea of continuing or coordinating them in the kitchen to avoid the choppy look that excessive flooring treatments can bring to a home. Finally, remember that when using tile or stone, sizable rooms need large plain pieces, as patterned smaller surfaces look inappropriate in scale and appear too busy. Larger tiles and slabs of flagstone, for example, are better suited for the roomy kitchen.

PAGE 45
No longer isolated to cold gray warehouses, concrete can now be stained, polished, and scored to create a durable, long-lasting work of art for the kitchen floor.

UPPER RIGHT
A creative combination of ceramic tile, marble, and granite borders are used to accentuate the scale and shape of this kitchen's impressive island.

LOWER RIGHT
Tumbled stone tiles, showcased in a variety of shapes, sizes, and colors, are imaginatively laid out to define the center of this rustic kitchen.

LOWER LEFT
An inset grid of stone tiles stands in stark contrast to the free-form shapes of this floor's flagstone slabs. As an underfoot focal point, it is outstanding.

LOWER RIGHT
Terrazzo, common to villas and palaces in Italy, also can be used in a contemporary setting. Here, contrasting colored terrazzo tiles mimic the modular precision of this modern kitchen.

UPPER RIGHT
Wooden floors work perfectly in the kitchen. Hard-wearing, durable and easy on the back and legs, they can be used in patterned designs bringing spectacular detail to the kitchen. Various colored and grained woods—oak, maple, and birch, for example—can be combined for spectacular results.

Selecting the best material for your kitchen floor requires a balancing act between its practical requirements and the decorative style you want to create. Vinyl and linoleum have their place in a home that requires a softer, quieter surface that is also low-maintenance and inexpensive. They are perfect for families with young children, as they cushion the inevitable falls and dropped dishes that come with children. Wood is also somewhat soft, making it easy on the back and legs of those who stand in the kitchen for prolonged periods of time. It offers a warm comfortable feel and works well with many decorative styles. However, it requires regular maintenance and must be kept sealed. Ceramic tile has always been popular in the kitchen because of its durability, easy maintenance, waterproof nature, and wide selection of styles and colors. Unfortunately, it can be hard on the legs and feet and, if not textured, is slick when wet. Stone can also be hard on the feet, is noisy and, depending on the variety, needs to be sealed for protection. It is hard-wearing, long-lasting, and makes a very strong statement of style, from rustic to truly elegant. From granite to travertine, limestone to marble, stone has become a very popular flooring material for the kitchen and throughout the home. In fact, its look is so sought-after that tile has been developed that replicates the look of stone for those desiring a less-expensive alternative for their floors.

LEFT AND OPPOSITE
Proof that multiple flooring materials can combine to create a remarkable look, this stunning kitchen floor joins black granite, cherry, and canterra stone with stainless-steel insets. Granite and stainless steel are repeated in the countertops to continue the floor's strong material statement.

Walls are more than background to a kitchen's design; they are an integral part of it. Through imaginative and creative treatments, walls envelop a kitchen in character and personality. They set the style for the rest of the room and play host to statements of color, texture, and pattern. Unlike most other rooms in the home, wall space in the kitchen can be limited. After all, by the time the cabinets, windows, doors, and appliances are placed, there is little wall space unclaimed. That makes the limited detail of walls more critical. Paint, tile, stone, wallpaper, and hand-applied finishes are just a few of the homeowner's options. Displays of art, collectibles, and hanging utensils can be used for added character.

VERTICALS

Kitchen walls work double duty as they stand in defense of the elements of kitchen warfare. Here, in a room where food splashes, heat and steam fills the air, and a barrage of bumps and bangs assault the walls, the protective value of their treatment is important to consider. By selecting

durable materials that are easily maintained while they add a distinctive style to the room, you will create a kitchen that is alive with character and also a pleasure in which to both work and play.

The walls offer a unique opportunity for varied detail as they are oftentimes segmented into many areas in the kitchen. The backsplash behind the stove and under the cabinets is oftentimes isolated from the areas surrounding windows, the larger walls, and the sections that frame the room's appliances and cupboards. Consider each of these as separate areas to add complementary distinctive detail. Keep in mind the advantages of the many options. Oil-based and gloss paint finishes are available in a rainbow of shades and are durable and easily cleaned. Tile offers limitless creative possibilities and is both hard-wearing and impervious to moisture. So, too, is granite; and its durability and easy maintenance make it a carefree, yet sophisticated choice. Plaster, wooden paneling, and treated glass are among other materials that line up to enhance these vertical surfaces of the kitchen.

PAGE 51
Surfacing from beneath ochre-colored plaster, mosaics and grids of richly colored tiles add extraordinary detail to the walls of this rustically flavored kitchen.

UPPER LEFT
When windows are left unadorned, borders, stencils, and unique treatments are effective ways to frame the views with character. Here, hand-painted grapevines bring a fanciful look to the otherwise plain walls surrounding the kitchen sink.

LOWER LEFT
A profusion of hand-painted tiles creates a fresh country feeling that is the essence of this highly detailed kitchen. Plain-colored upper walls, a large solid-topped island, and a large unadorned window provide the relief needed to keep the patterned tiles from becoming visually overwhelming.

OPPOSITE
When limited to a single wall in the kitchen, distinctive surface treatments like this chiseled stone and polished marble can create a striking focal point. Used more broadly, the treatments become overpowering and less effective aesthetically.

A focal point in many kitchens, the backsplash is like a magnet to over-the-top detail. Tile is one of the most popular materials used in this area because it is impervious to steam and moisture, while it is also easily cleaned. The endless colors, textures, sizes, and shapes of tile add to its appeal. Color-washed, solid, or hand-painted designs can be used solo or mixed and matched. From geometrically placed squares to sculpted ceramic borders and stunning mosaic images, the possibilities are limitless. When designing this feature, consider incorporating unique hooks or racks for placing utensils, spices, or cookware, keeping them close at hand while working.

OPPOSITE
The artist of this vibrant mosaic uses chips, shards, and full-sized tiles of assorted thickness and textures to create a seemingly three-dimensional design. The result is a brilliant backsplash that captures the festive, carefree feel of this tropical vacation home.

Like a vacant canvas suspended overhead, the ceiling is one of the most overlooked opportunities for creative detail in the kitchen. Even in the simplest of kitchens, it has enormous decorative potential. Color and texture can bring it to life. Stencils and moldings can dress its edges while imaginative lighting, hanging chandeliers, ceiling fans, pot racks, and even twirling mobiles can hang from it like brilliant jewelry. More elaborately architectural kitchens can boast sculpted and contoured ceilings that are enhanced with dramatic beams, inset skylights, or carved wooden panels.

OVERHEAD

Polished planking, pressed tin, and hand-applied frescoes, among other treatments, can also be used to adorn the ceiling's surface. The potential for individualized expression is enormous. Furthermore, in a room in which cabinetry and appliances claim wall space, islands and fixtures interrupt flooring patterns, and countertops are kept clear for food preparation, the ceiling is the one surface in the room that is unencumbered with working essentials, leaving it open to your personalized decorative detailing. Look upward and let your creativity fly as you use the ceiling to add to your kitchen's style.

Once you recognize the enormous contribution a detailed ceiling can make to the flavor of the kitchen, your own overhead surface will inspire your own treatment of detail. The simplest means of ceiling decoration is color. You can visually send the ceiling skyward with pale shades or bring it downward with bold, dark colors. Stencils, molding, and hand-painted images can enhance a traditionally styled kitchen, while high-wire halogen lights, broad skylights, and colored illumination make an impact on contemporary spaces. Even detail from below can effect the ceiling, as up-lights and wall sconces that shine upward send a play of light and shadow, giving the ceiling character and personality during the evening hours. Shine them through the branches of potted plants and the ceiling becomes patterned like a sun-dappled jungle floor.

PAGE 57
To underscore the impressive architecture of this dramatic kitchen, an enchanting landscape decorates the contoured ceiling with color and character. The image draws the eye upward and provides added dimension to the beautiful overhead surface.

PAGES 58–59
Oftentimes, high voluminous ceilings can appear vacant and distant, leaving the room with an empty cavernous feeling. Detail can be used to bring them into reach. Structural as well as simple surface treatments—beams, wooden panels, and layered colors for example—are effective ways to highlight overhead architecture while giving it a spatially comfortable feel.

LEFT
In a kitchen where every surface is brilliantly detailed, the ceiling is not left untouched. An inset box of vibrant color, framed with a heavy molding, complements the more intricately textured glass-mosaic backsplash, striated-glass cabinet fronts, and stacked-stone walls.

RIGHT
Any surface can benefit from unique detail. This architecturally plain ceiling is boldly covered with period stamped-copper panels giving it a warm, reflective quality that is in keeping with the style of the kitchen. Molding frames the treatment beautifully.

As the kitchen has evolved in the present-day home, so, too, have its cabinets. Yesterday's featureless, wall-mounted "boxes" are a thing of the past. Today, cabinets are designed and finished like fine pieces of furniture. Elaborately fashioned surfaces are lavished with hand-carved details and art-like hardware. Bases are oftentimes raised on curved legs like those of antique armoires. Imaginative door fronts—etched glass, iron grids, and pressed-tin panels for example—add enormous character to the fixtures, as do hand-rubbed, distressed, crackled, and antiqued

CABINETS

finishes. And these describe only wooden cabinets. Aluminum, stainless steel, and laminates are among the many other materials creatively used. Of course, the choice of material and finish strongly influences the mood and style of the kitchen. This decision should also influence the selection of countertop materials paired with the cabinets. Clearly, butcher block, tile, granite, and stainless steel contribute to a distinct look as well. Further, combining two or more cabinet finishes, as well as countertop surfaces, in a room can be an effective way to avoid the sometimes-overwhelming effect of a room smothered in a single treatment.

To the functionally minded, cabinets are essential for providing much-needed storage in the kitchen. But to those who aspire for more, cabinets offer an opportunity to add enormous design and detail to their personalized kitchens.

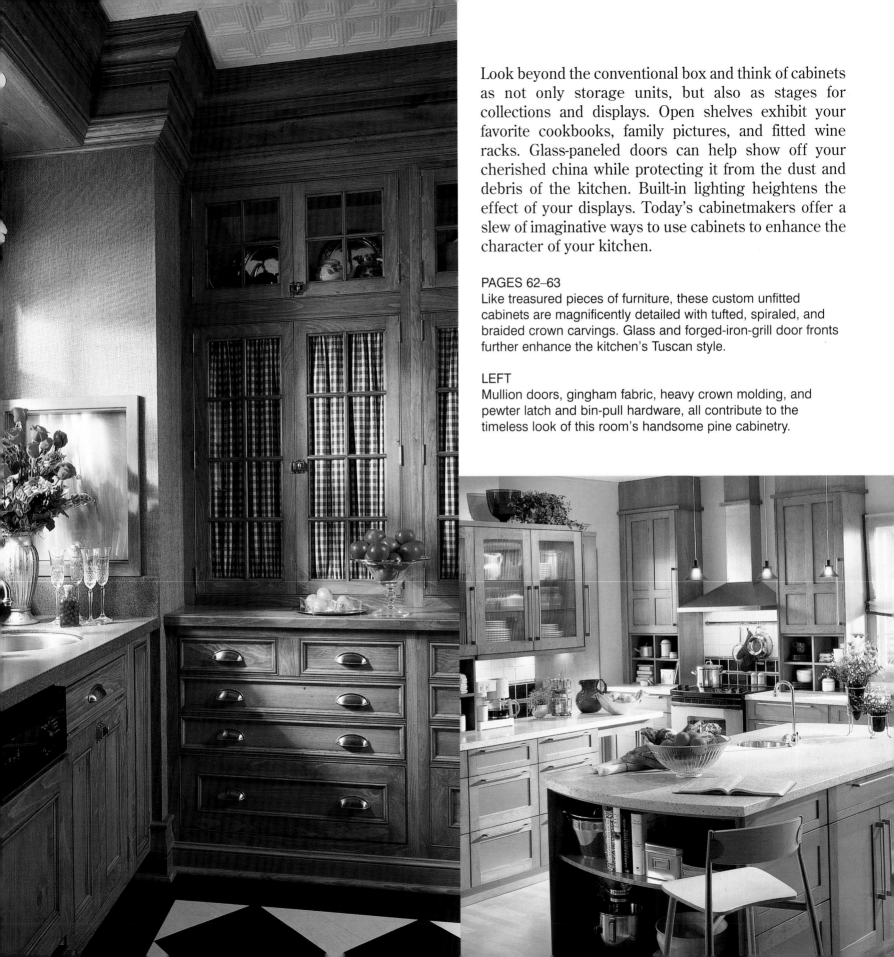

Look beyond the conventional box and think of cabinets as not only storage units, but also as stages for collections and displays. Open shelves exhibit your favorite cookbooks, family pictures, and fitted wine racks. Glass-paneled doors can help show off your cherished china while protecting it from the dust and debris of the kitchen. Built-in lighting heightens the effect of your displays. Today's cabinetmakers offer a slew of imaginative ways to use cabinets to enhance the character of your kitchen.

PAGES 62–63
Like treasured pieces of furniture, these custom unfitted cabinets are magnificently detailed with tufted, spiraled, and braided crown carvings. Glass and forged-iron-grill door fronts further enhance the kitchen's Tuscan style.

LEFT
Mullion doors, gingham fabric, heavy crown molding, and pewter latch and bin-pull hardware, all contribute to the timeless look of this room's handsome pine cabinetry.

In the "fitted" kitchen, continuous cabinets hug the walls from end to end. They are very efficient in small kitchens and are also used in many contemporary settings because of their seamless look. "Unfitted" cabinets, on the other hand, provide a less structured and more casual feel. Oftentimes, handcrafted and custom-made, they are placed in the kitchen at various heights and depths, giving the appearance of one-of-a-kind freestanding furniture pieces. The look is particularly appealing in open floor plans as the individualized style flows into the dining and living areas that are home to similar-looking furnishings.

OPPOSITE LOWER AND BELOW
Glass-front cabinets are dynamic in all settings. Whether they are used with striated glass in a contemporary room or like an antique hutch in a traditional space, they add interest and character while displaying and storing your glassware and dishes.

RIGHT
Heavily carved maple cabinets bring the Old World flavor of Mexico into this kitchen. Canterra stone floors and handwrought-iron accessories strengthen the look.

Functionally, decorative hardware serves to open, close, and secure the doors and drawers throughout the kitchen. Stylistically, these handles, knobs, hinges, and other pieces are the "jewels" that dress the room's cabinets and fixtures. The thoughtful selection of hardware is very important because of its power to alter the look and style of the kitchen. It can help define a country design with wood or porcelain pulls or, just as easily, provide a striking modern edge with sculpted steel or colored glass handles. In historic kitchens, the inclusion of era-appropriate pieces can be the clincher in creating an authentic period look.

From artistic to antique designs, there are endless options when choosing hardware for the kitchen. As long as you are sensitive to the character of the room, there are no rules to bind your selections. Savor the exciting options and keep in mind there may be more than one look that is perfect for your personalized space. What's more, nothing says you have to limit yourself to a single design. Using more than one style of hardware in a kitchen can add dramatic character. In the kitchen on this page, the multiple forms and finishes of its cabinetry are accentuated with an assortment of hardware pieces. Simple bronze balls, cut-glass knobs, and rustic drop pulls punctuate the room's bold style.

The "basic ingredients," or essential elements, of a kitchen can help shape its personality and character. In the past, these functional components of the kitchen were created and used with little thought to design. Boxy appliances, plain countertops and harsh lighting screamed of utilitarian sameness. Now it is sometimes hard to tell whether these items are selected for their practical purposes or for the flair and panache they bring to the room. Take today's appliances, for instance. Designed to seduce with their stylish good looks, they are offered in an array of spectacular finishes and shapes. Their features and gadgets intrigue and tempt even those individuals who find boiling water a challenging recipe. Of course, it would be criminal to place these striking appliances in a kitchen where the other essentials were not stylized. Richly surfaced countertops and a myriad of sources for both task and ambient lighting help set the stage for a wonderfully detailed kitchen. As always, keep your eye on your priorities and functional needs before giving in to the temptations these items present. A well-designed and detailed kitchen should be enjoyed by the services, as well as the sights, it provides.

Appliances are the true laborers of the kitchen. Some are essential, some are helpful, and still others are simply indulgent. The indispensables to every kitchen are the refrigerator/freezer, the stove, and the oven. The remaining appliances are selected based on their importance to the live-in chefs of the home. By their sheer number and size, appliances combine to make a dominant statement in the style and design direction of the kitchen. Their bulk, colors, and finishes can be either muted to subtly blend into the room, or boldly stated to become exclamation points throughout the space. This is detail at work. Do you want the drama that bright hues and a brilliant sheen present, or do you prefer the understated effect of appliances disguised to blend into surrounding cabinetry? The decorative options are mesmerizing. Refrigerator fronts range from the basic white to sophisticated black, warm wood to stainless steel, and even glass that allows you to see the contents without opening the door. Ovens are offered with similar options. The configurations offered are dizzying. Double ovens, gas and electric ranges, built-in grills, steamers and warmers, all add to the appliance's options. And

APPLIANCES

the vent hood has certainly evolved from a boxy necessity. In many kitchens it has become an art form. While appliances may be some of the hardest working elements in the kitchen, that doesn't mean they can't get dressed-up for the job.

Beyond its decorative intrigue, much of a kitchen's appeal lies in its efficiency. The selection and positioning of appliances strongly affects the functional ease of the space. While kitchen planning is as individualistic as the people who use the room, there is an accepted plan for a well-designed space. Described as a working triangle, this plan places the sink, the stove, and the refrigerator respectively at the three points of a triangle. These working elements should be within a few steps of each other but not so close as to constrict movement while cooking. A general guide, this theory adjusts to the size and shape of the kitchen, as well as the planning desires of the individual homeowners.

PAGES 70–71
Unique appliances can add immense character to a kitchen, while others are best left understated or disguised behind cabinet fronts. This welcoming country kitchen illustrates this theory by proudly displaying a handsome retro stove while hiding the neighboring dishwasher behind a panel that appears to be a series of bin-handled drawers.

UPPER LEFT AND LOWER RIGHT
From the stamped ceiling to the cherry floors, this richly detailed kitchen reflects vintage Victorian character at every turn. Spectacular green and chrome HeartLand® appliances are incorporated to enhance, without distracting from, the well-executed design.

OPPOSITE
To draw the eye into this detail-rich kitchen, a trompe l'oeil pantry scene adorns refrigerator doors with spectacular results.

In many kitchens, the ventilation hood is one of the strongest focal points simply because of its sheer size and placement. Add imaginative detail and it draws the eye like a magnet. As seen on these pages this appliance can be created from an endless combination of intriguing materials and treatments. Sleek aluminum, curvaceous plaster, handmade tile and hammered copper are just the beginning of the many elements used to transform this ordinary working object into a work of art. Its size, shape, and positioning in the room are also open to the ingenuity of design. While certainly the vent hood was functionally engineered to remove excess heat and moisture from the cooking area, its visual impact in today's kitchen makes it as much a decorative element as a working appliance.

The countertop is hands down the hardest working surface in the kitchen. And through all the chopping, dicing, spilling, wiping, and heat it takes on a daily basis, it is expected to look as good as the pampered tabletops found elsewhere in the home. That is a tall order! There are a number of options for this work surface that includes granite, slate, ceramic tile, stainless steel, wood, laminates, and even waxed concrete. Each of these has specific features that can benefit an active kitchen.

COUNTERTOPS

They also have visual strengths that impact the style of the room. Granite favors a sophisticated, polished look. Wood adds warmth and richness. Tile, which is itself a form of art, offers the opportunity to truly express one's personal style through brilliant color and uniquely detailed designs. Of course, stainless steel leans toward a contemporary, professional appearance. The key to successfully

selecting your countertop surface is to first consider the functional merits of your selections and then evaluate their place in your design scheme. Remember, too, that the use of more than one countertop treatment in the kitchen can be effective. An island with a butcher-block top, for example, can beautifully complement nearby stone or tiled countertops, bringing a creatively executed look to your room.

Using multiple countertop materials throughout a kitchen has its advantages. First, the contrasting colors, textures, and patterns of the varied surfaces lend interest and intrigue to the room. Second, because no single material performs perfectly for all cooking and food preparation tasks, different elements are chosen and positioned for the specific benefits they offer. Wood favors chopping and slicing, while stainless steel, high-quality laminate, and other water-resilient materials are better near the sink. The heatproof nature of tile, granite, and stainless steel make them ideal near the stove. Of course, marble makes the perfect nonstick surface for the serious pastry chef kneading his pastry dough.

Determining the style for the edge of your kitchen countertops is akin to selecting a frame for a beautiful painting. Both accentuate the work of art they surround as they add to the overall style of the room in which they are used. For solid slab surfaces like granite, a clean or bullnose edge is fitting for a contemporary setting. A broken or chiseled edge can also work here, giving an artsy rugged look. A beveled, sculpted, or carved profile is magnificent in a traditional or transitional setting. Tile works in all settings and its edges can be understated with matching edges or feature compelling sculpted, braided, and relief trims. Using a contrasting color or differently sized tiles draws the eye to the edge of the counter and away from the simpler field of tile it borders. Butcher block, stainless steel, concrete, and other options also have edges that invite creative interpretation. As seen on these pages, the counter-top edge is just one more element of the design that can add substantial character to your kitchen.

PAGE 77
The "broken" edges of this kitchen's granite countertops and breakfast bar stand in striking contrast to the center island's smooth butcher-block surface. In combination, they complement the room's texture-rich nature.

Do you find yourself traveling from area to area when cooking in your kitchen? Are you short of storage space? Do you end up looking into a wall or having your back to your company while cooking? The solution to these problems is the centrally located kitchen island. The anchor of a busy kitchen, the island is a multi-talented fixture that provides a working surface and pivotal location for preparing food while helping to stylistically shape the room. Many of today's islands are spectacularly designed in both the form and functions they provide. Alluring silhouettes, multilevel surfaces, and varied head-turning materials are imaginatively combined. Built-in wine racks, adjustable shelving, rinsing sinks, cooktops, and warming drawers are just a number of the "bells and whistles" that accompany the well-equipped island. Attached eating bars are included to invite casual dining as well as company for the cook. Keeping the island appropriately scaled to the rest of the kitchen is important. Many islands appear too large for the kitchen in which they are placed. An island should not be so big as to hinder movement in the room or visually bully the space with its size. Like cabinetry, it should be considered a piece of furniture that is thoughtfully integrated into the space and design of the room.

OPPOSITE
Separate islands, designed for a distinctive purpose, set the stage for multichef, gourmet cooking. Each island is outfitted with its own unique features and countertop material to support the functions for which it was created.

LEFT
Like a piece of a puzzle, this island was custom-shaped to fit the undulating curves of this kitchen's countertops. A distressed finish, built-in shelves, and rinsing sink add to its appeal.

LOWER LEFT
To capture a breathtaking view, upper cabinets are eliminated and replaced with this storage-rich center island. Its black granite top and diagonally set cherry wood siding enhance the rich, sophisticated look of the room.

LOWER RIGHT
A classic country-styled kitchen houses a simple, yet feature-loaded island. A contrasting colored, beaded backing gives dimension to the built-in shelves.

The lighting in today's kitchen does more than brighten the room's working surfaces. With a flip of a switch, it can wash the space with warmth, cause the crystal to sparkle, and make the room's colors and textures come alive. Light defines the kitchen, giving it a sense of space while emphasizing the details that create the room's character. No

LIGHTING

matter how beautifully designed the kitchen, without good lighting, its décor and personality cannot be fully developed. Good lighting truly makes the difference between a kitchen that appears flat and unappealing to one that is vital and dynamic. As the kitchen has evolved, it has grown from a workroom with overhead fluorescent tubes to a multifunctional space home to varied types of lighting. The key to effectively incorporating light into your kitchen is to foremost consider the many purposes of the room. Give the room strong overall lighting and then, for cooking and food preparation, brighten work areas with light that focuses on the task-oriented zones. Finally, create ambience by adding decorative lighting to spotlight the room's unique details, finishing touches, and accessories. Keep in mind, there are two parts to every source of light you consider. First, the fixture itself—its texture, shape, material, and color—influences the character of the space. Second, the quality and direction of the light it produces, spreads, reflects, and spots also make a strong statement of style in the room.

In the kitchen, where lighting is very important for both practical and design-oriented reasons, different types of light are employed based on varied needs and wants of the homeowners. There are a number of categories of lighting that address different needs. Of course, the simplest and most loved source of light is natural—the sun. Well-placed windows and skylights harness this favored source as it brings life to the kitchen, at least during the daylight hours. Given a choice, no kitchen should be without it. A man-made source of background illumination is ambient, or general, lighting. It is used to create an overall level of light in the room. It can be created by a number of contributing sources. Overhead fixtures, decorative sconces, and torchéres that reflect or diffuse light off the room's surfaces create the general light by which we see. Task lighting, on the other hand, addresses work-specific lighting needs and is key to a well-designed kitchen. If you have ever tried to cook under dim lights or fixtures that throw misdirected shadows and hot spots, you know how important this localized type of lighting is. Under cupboard lights, recessed halogens, and desk lamps are examples of this work-oriented source of light. Finally, accent or spot lighting is used aesthetically to highlight wall art, decorative objects or specific points of interest in the room. Often dimmable, these lights help set the kitchen's mood and are the artist's most creative strokes of lighting that finish the overall style of the space. While light itself is a decorative detail that aesthetically renders style to the kitchen, so, too, do its sources. Look beyond the basic fluorescent tubes. Consider endless options from chandeliers to wire strung halogens, shaded lamps to ornate sconces.

Multiple sources of light contribute to the warm inviting atmosphere of this beautiful kitchen (opposite). The overhead chandelier (right) displays a strong regional style while providing general lighting that can be brightened or dimmed by the turn of a dial. Undercounter lighting showcases the textured backsplash and countertops as it delivers direct light for cooking and food preparation tasks (lower left). Uplights on the pot shelves emphasize the room's lofty architecture, while a simple shaded lamp (lower right) directs the eye into the room with its golden pool of light.

PAGE 82
Symmetrically hung in a row, a succession of stainless-steel pendants perform as both decorative art and light sources. Functionally, these six fixtures light the work surface of the long granite countertop much more effectively than would one or two larger lights.

Because of the built-in nature of the kitchen and its furnishings, lighting is most often a fixed decorative element. Overhead mounts, spots, recessed lighting, and fixtures are permanently installed to coordinate with steadfast cabinetry and task areas. However, there are a number of ways to add flexibility to the room's lighting. Dimmers can be attached to a fixture facilitating the adjustment of its light's intensity. Dimmers can change the ambience of the kitchen and its quantity of light at a moment's notice. Small table lamps and accent lights, placed in cupboards and nooks, are also effective ways to illuminate a kitchen with adjustable light. Even a distinctive, decorative sconce or up-lights in potted plants can change the character of the room as they throw shapes and shadows on its ceiling surface.

OPPOSITE
Large open floor plans need strong lighting statements to unify the extended spaces. Wires of overhead halogen lights span the kitchen and dramatically accentuate the size and style of the entire room.

LEFT AND BELOW
Overhead recessed halogens, discreet undercounter illumination, and a series of hand-blown amber glass pendants combine to create an engaging versatile lighting arrangement for this active kitchen.

There is no greater gift to a kitchen than natural light. It warms the space in the morning and constantly changes the feel of the room throughout the day. As the sun moves across the sky, our perception of the kitchen's colors, textures, and overall ambience changes with the amount of natural light the room receives. A yellow wall bathed in sunlight, for instance, can seem muted and golden when shadowed or indirectly illuminated. Textures, too, appear more or less obvious, depending on the play of light and shadow on their surfaces. Knowing this, selecting colors and textures for the kitchen should be done in the room during different times of the day as well as under the artificial light used at night.

The direction from which the light comes affects the feel of the room. In the northern hemisphere, light from the north is cooler and whiter than the golden, warmer light that streams though south-oriented windows. The light from the south is a more constant sweeping light. Windows are the most common way to welcome natural light into the space. In a room where cabinetry and appliances occupy so much of the valued wall space, the placement and decoration of windows is one this room's most significant, and sometimes challenging, decorative details. In many kitchens, the over-the-sink window is most important because as it welcomes light in, it also provides a view out. French, large single-pained, or sliding glass doors to the outside also can do this. In spatially challenged kitchens, smaller windows below the cabinets or above pot shelves can help capture daylight, while they also become interesting detail for the room. Skylights, too, are a wonderful way to embrace natural light. When placed directly over a center island or task station, they provide abundant clear light for daytime cooking.

OPPOSITE
An expansive window and large overhead skylight provide two substantial openings that invite the brilliant light of this room. Throughout the day, the room's light is more consistent and less varied than that of a room with only a single source of natural light.

RIGHT
The quality of light in the kitchen is impacted by the room's window treatments and the color and texture of its surfaces. White walls and ceilings, semitransparent blinds, and reflective surfaces softly splay light throughout this tranquil room (upper right). A myriad of objects and surfaces come alive when hit by the natural light from this kitchen window. Pull-back draperies and a simple blind filter the light, yet can also give complete privacy when desired (center right). The vitality and decorative strength of this colorful wall and paneled wainscoting is a credit to the play of sunlight and shadows across its surface (lower right).

If you have an appetite for style, the kitchen is the perfect place to use detail to bring personality and character into your home. "Spicing" kitchen décor with engaging elements that reflect your personal taste can create a look that is uniquely yours. There are many ways to do this. One of these is the use of imaginative accessories. They are the flavorful items—some decorative, others practical—that bring points of interest and character to the kitchen. They can be peppered throughout—mounted on walls, stacked on shelves, set on tables and shown-off through glass-front cabinets. Accessories are the seasonings of the décor—cherished collectibles, distinctive cookware, and handpicked knickknacks to name a few. Through their form, character, and art of display, they add immeasurably to the character of the kitchen.

Color also adds infinity to the room's personality, with its vivid hues and soft pastels. Properly chosen, it is savored every time someone enters the space. Go ahead; determine the direction of your decorative recipe and experiment with the many "condiments" that when added, a pinch here or a tad there, spice your kitchen with a flavor that is distinctively yours.

Accessories are the storytellers of the home. They mutely speak of the individuals who live in a space, divulging their interests, tastes, travels, and loves. And because the well-designed kitchen is a haven to personal comfort and expression, it is no wonder that it is also home to so many of these tell-all details. Accessories define an immense number of decorative and practical items that, in the kitchen, can be found at every turn—pottery, glassware, baskets, sculpture, wall

ACCESSORIES

hangings, paintings, photographs, and floral arrangements, to name just a few. Some are purely decorative like the grape-stake wreath hung on the kitchen door. Others, like the colorful biscotti jar, are functional in use; however, their true contribution lies in the charm and flavor they bring to the space. What both of these pieces have in common is their ability to enrich the kitchen with a unique and personal style. Select your accessories like a storyteller chooses words. Opt for items that have special meaning to you or that specifically contribute to the theme you desire. Be careful, though. Superfluous accessories, like redundant words, can weaken the tale told and actually distract from those that have singular meaning and importance. When you accessorize your kitchen, simply determine the narrative you want the room to tell and creatively pen the story with special items of color, style, and flair.

RIGHT
Taking its textural and color cues from the rugged earth, this kitchen's raw sensuous beauty is enhanced by its distinctive accessories. The coarse woven basket, chiseled stone and wooden bowls, and thriving pencil plant, all flatter the pattern-rich granite countertop and tile backsplash.

OPPOSITE UPPER LEFT
Casual pockets of accessory groupings owe their interest to a combination of unlike objects. Carved wooden figures, terracotta jugs, glazed pottery, and brightly painted dishware unite to adorn this handsome relaxed kitchen.

OPPOSITE LOWER LEFT
In the kitchen, functional tools and utensils often make the most striking accessories. Everyday objects like this bulky scale, and wooden mortar and pestle become eye-catching when their properties—shape, finish, and color—create visual interest in the room.

The kitchen's pot shelves, architectural niches, glass-front cabinets, and abundant countertop surfaces are magnets for eye-catching accessories. Many of these are kitchen tools. Dishware, glassware, pitchers, utensils, and cookware play dual roles. A bright green mixing bowl, a copper double boiler, and a jar of wooden utensils become accessories when their unique qualities enhance the style and flavor of the kitchen. Purely decorative items also have a place here. Pictures on the walls, architectural remnants on the shelves, and glass sculptures on the tabletop are finishing touches that add to the room's personality.

When selecting accessories, foremost they should be interesting and compelling to you. Sometimes a common bowl may have a finish or shape that is stimulating. A picture may conjure up memories or a platter may be glazed with your favorite hue. When grouped, many items also become captivating. Shelves of bubbled-glass highballs, for example, become a spectacle under bright overhead lights.

Consider the qualities of your accessories when introducing them into the kitchen. They should complement the style of the room. Their size, shape, texture, and color, all influence their compatibility with the space. Their appeal may be in the way that they blend into the room or it may be the strong contrast they present. Earthy rustic kitchens favor natural, heavy, and substantial accessories. Tiny bric-a-brac is not suitable here. On the other hand, a refined elegant kitchen does not welcome rough-hewn and bullying items. Of course, there are always exceptions. A handcarved wooden bowl may flatter a similarly unrefined tile countertop, yet be equally as attractive contrasting with a contemporary polished-granite surface. Trial and error is the key.

*Have nothing in your houses
that you do not know to be
useful,*

or believe to be beautiful.

William Morris

Collections and displays link a person to his or her home as they truly reflect the individual's style and taste. This holds true particularly in today's kitchen. Here, shelves, glass-front cabinets, and corner cupboards house favored items. So, too, do pot shelves, walls, countertops, and architectural niches. Even the windowsill above the sink is not safe from the gathering of worthy pieces. The collected objects do not have to be costly or rare. In fact, what would be out-of-place or inappropriate for display elsewhere in the house becomes the

DISPLAY

perfect accent when artistically integrated into the kitchen. Everyday dishes, pottery, and utensils of intriguing design and character are as suitable for display here as is a crystal vase in an elegant living room. The charm of commonly used items seems to come alive in the kitchen.

The key to selecting the objects you display should be based on their meaning to you and the magic they bring to your kitchen. Do the pieces reveal your likes and interests? Do they complement the feel of the room? When combined, do they make an aesthetically appealing statement? When objects are grouped and displayed together, there are endless ways to arrange them throughout the kitchen; however, all well-designed compositions share a common character. They combine organization with interest, enticing an admirer to get closer to appreciate each piece individually. For what is a beautiful collection but the sum of its beautiful parts?

The color, shape, and finish of an object help define it. So do its texture and size. These are the properties that can make even the most utilitarian and simple item interesting. A hand-glazed yellow platter, for instance, becomes art when hanging on the wall. A stack of thick-edged dishes of varying colors appears sculptural. Even simple clear-glass canisters, sparkling under a sunny window or bright halogen light produce a striking statement. There is so much visual strength that can be found in the room's most basic items. When carefully selected and arranged, they can create magic.

Use repetition, texture, scale, and color as tools in display. Five stacked bowls take on new life when individually lined up at regular intervals. A primitive wooden tray paired with brilliant glassware successfully plays upon the contrasting finishes of each. Even a collection of matching dishes becomes interesting when dissimilarities in size or shape are punctuated in presentation.

Give display room to breathe and do not clutter or pile items together. When choosing pieces, rule nothing out. Consider every object and look for qualities that you may not have recognized before. Use trial and error, grouping and regrouping, until you create a statement of style that enriches your kitchen and speaks of your own individual taste.

PAGE 99
Architectural niches are the ideal stage for displaying dramatic decorative accessories. The backs of this kitchen's overhead niches are painted with a contrasting color to add even more eye-catching detail.

OPPOSITE
Repetition, arresting shapes, and a disciplined placement of items combine to give this kitchen's open-shelf display dramatic impact.

BELOW
A large arrangement of similarly colored pieces focuses on the contrasting sizes and shapes of the individual items to attain its appeal. It is best to group these items rather than spread them throughout the room.

RIGHT
A collection of hand-painted dishes is boldly displayed in open lighted shelves. The least used pieces are vertically staged on the upper shelves. The more frequently handled items are stacked below, making them easy to use while effortlessly adding visual interest to the overall presentation.

The pragmatic use them for extra storage, while the creative see them as one more way to detail their kitchen. Of course, both are correct. Hanging fixtures—racks, hooks, and assorted dangling contraptions—all provide a way to clear the countertops of clutter while providing unique character to the room. Most well known, the hanging rack was traditionally used as

HANGING ON

a practical fixture for the accessible storage of cookware, utensils, and food. Today it has evolved into one of the most decorative accessories in the kitchen. Along with its many forms and fabrications, its uniqueness has grown with the imaginative array of objects suspended from its structure. Dangling dried flowers, bundled herbs, ropes of garlic, and chili ristras join the token saucepan. Whimsical pottery, copper molds, and even treasured toys add color, texture, and amusement. Simple hooks also provide showy storage for cups beneath cupboards, utensils over cooktops, and pots above stoves. Even the kitchen's light fixture is susceptible to hanging doodads and kitchen tools.

In an overly large cavernous kitchen, the hanging rack can help fill overwhelming space above and give the room a more comfortable feel. The rack can be custom-made to mimic the shape of an island below and can be forged from one or more materials. From handwrought iron to sleek stainless steel combined with bleached wood, today's hanging rack can be designed to fit any style of kitchen. Classic kitchens may boast hanging copper molds, iron cookware, and dried herbs. Contemporary racks may dangle shiny stainless-steel cookware and utensils. The options are endless and open to interpretation. Small kitchens also benefit from hanging fixtures and under-counter hooks. These help keep the limited counter space free for cooking and relieve the pressure for storage of kitchen essentials. Doubling up on function and aesthetics, the hanging fixture is a gift to the spatially challenged room.

PAGE 102
A coffee-table base becomes a unique overhead rack when attached to this kitchen's ceiling. Decorative metal bars are added to provide hanging rods for assorted pots and pans.

OPPOSITE
The sky is the limit when it comes to the imaginative use of hanging details in the kitchen. A fanciful chandelier is laden with decorative kitchen ornaments tied beneath shaded teacup lights (upper left). A country wreath hangs from above, echoing the comforting natural style of the room (upper right). A collage of colorful peppers and copper cookware festively hang from this rustic Mexican-style rack (center). Plates collected from worldly travels evoke memories and create colorful display when mounted about the room (lower left). Nothing is off-limits when this homeowner's handmade wooden canoe finds itself hanging above the rustic character-filled kitchen (lower right).

Framed watercolors and boldly colored canvases are not the sole property of the living room or gallery hall. The kitchen can also reap the benefits of these wonderful accessories. The challenge is finding the room and appropriate spot to place them in an area already short of wall space. What's more, they should be displayed out of the way of the steam, splattered food, and splashing liquids common to most kitchens. Occasionally, there is a large blank wall that can house a large canvas. This provides a perfect opportunity to create a strong statement of color and style. By sheer size, the impact of a large image can cause it to become a major focal point in the room. It can help direct the color, story, and theme of the room. Smaller images, when grouped together can have the same effect. Individually, smaller framed art also can be mounted on the walls or displayed like many other accessories. Be imaginative—try them under cabinets, inside lighted cupboards, and staged with other favorites in niches and on pot shelves. The overall effect may be a work of art.

OPPOSITE
A large framed oil painting of glazed pottery sets the tone for this elegantly detailed kitchen. Smaller framed watercolors are intermingled with other accessories, creating charming pockets of display throughout the room.

UPPER RIGHT
Safely positioned away from the cooking area of the kitchen, this colorful and compelling art becomes the room's main focal point.

LOWER LEFT
The vacant countertop of an understated kitchen provides rich opportunity for staging art. Against a more ornate background, the visual impact made by this pair of portraits would be lessened dramatically.

The kitchen has become home to some of the most ingenious fixtures and accents. They have been designed to help the space operate smoothly while, at the same time, adding a distinctive sense of style and flavor to the room. Boxy storage drawers have evolved

WORKING ACCENTS

into woven-wicker baskets and glass-front bins. Nondescript cabinetry opens up into full self-service bars, mobile service carts, and consolidated chef pantries. Televisions appear out of nowhere as they ascend from compartments built into countertops and center islands. Sound systems and operating panels are hidden behind doors and above cabinets. Even common utensils are arranged on specially designed racks, creating a statement of art as well as one of practicality. The common denominator between these and endless other ingenious kitchen fixtures is simply imagination. It turns the most ordinary objects into extraordinary decorative details.

Remember the mood rings of the 1970s? When you put them on, they turned different colors supposedly based on your disposition. While their value as jewelry is highly questionable, the concept of tying colors to moods is indisputable. Phrases like "feeling blue," "green with envy," and "red-hot tempers," all attest to this connection. In the home, color is by far the most powerful element of design, guaranteed to bring emotion and character to everything it tints. Whether you are aware of it or not, there is nowhere in your home that color does not touch you.

COLOR

It transforms even the smallest detail with its ability to mold moods, create feelings, and enrich its surroundings. In the kitchen, it can be found throughout—from the paint on the walls and glaze on the tile to the yarns of the rug and the finishes on the room's endless accessories. Of course, the decision about incorporating color into the kitchen is highly individual as it is based on one's personality. While one person may thrive on the subtle hues of ivory marble, another may require the intensity of walls saturated with sunflower-yellow paint. Some people flourish in a calm relaxing environment, while others require the excitement and stimulation of high-energy surroundings. Some turn a mood ring blue, others turn it red. Such is the science of color!

Color brings life and character to everything it touches. It is by far the most potent tool of design. In the kitchen, it can soothe as it subtly influences the muted tones of waxed woods, polished granite, and hand-rubbed hardware. On the other hand, hue bright walls, heavily glazed tiles, and boldly woven rugs energize with color's more vibrant power. No one is indifferent to color. Some dream of a kitchen with a soft mellow setting, others prefer a bright animated space, and still others desire a neutral room that acts as a backdrop to more robustly tinted accents. In any case, color is key to creating the "ideal" kitchen.

Before you open the kitchen door to color, there are a few points you should consider. Of course, there is the purpose of your kitchen and the ambience you want it to have. Generally, comfortable welcoming colors are more suitable than strong overwhelming colors for rooms in which you plan to spend long periods of time. Powerful dynamic colors on the other hand, are better experienced in shorter spurts of time. Are there lighting and spatial challenges in your kitchen? Color can directly impact the dimensional feel of the space. Lighter hues can expand a small room while deeper tones close it in, causing a smaller more intimate perception of the area. Lighting also affects the sense of space and powerfully accentuates the way color is perceived. A color seen under direct sunlight is entirely different than the same color swathed with soft lamplight. It is wise to view a color in the various "lights of the day" before deciding on its inclusion.

Foremost, you must decide how you want the room to feel—cozy, warm, energetic, brilliant, mellow, or soothing. Cool colors like blues and greens make a room seem larger while giving it a relaxed calming atmosphere. Warmer color—yellows, reds, and oranges—on the other hand, cause a room to appear cozier and closer. These are but a handful of sensations that color influences. While there are volumes of books written on the practical and emotional use of color in the home, the key is to select a palette that makes you smile and brings a sense of comfort and personal style to your kitchen.

I cannot pretend to feel impartial about colours. I rejoice with the brilliant ones and am genuinely sorry for the poor browns.

Winston Churchill

PAGE 110
Bold yellow walls and purple fitted cabinets contribute to the stimulating feel of this lively kitchen. Beautiful antique rugs are used to tie the complementary colors together.

PAGE 112 LOWER LEFT
High-energy apple green creates the perfect backdrop for this contemporary kitchen. Large open floor plans can accommodate bold colors without becoming overwhelmed by their strength.

PAGE 112 UPPER RIGHT
Bright chrome-yellow cabinetry sets the tone for this energetic kitchen. When paired with black, the color becomes even stronger and more intense. A suspended white ceiling balances with the room's vibrant color preventing it from becoming overpowering.

PAGE 113 LOWER LEFT
Blue and white are the perfect partners to bring a fresh soothing atmosphere to a room. Golden wooden floors, brass hardware, and touches of yellow throughout add warmth to the otherwise cool color story.

PAGE 113 UPPER RIGHT
The intensity of this kitchen's stunning crimson cabinetry is kept in check by the large expanse of windows overlooking a desert preserve. Black granite accentuates the room's dynamic red wood and stylized stainless-steel hardware.

There are many ways to introduce color to your kitchen. For a temporary and isolated splash of color, a bowl of oranges, a vase of brilliant sunflowers, or a stack of cerulean blue dish towels can do the trick. While they are not part of the room's "color plan," they punctuate the kitchen with their fresh, eye-catching brilliance. They are invigorating, yet fleeting color statements capable of being changed at a moment's notice. This is part of their charm.

Accent colors are a more coordinated, less transient way to include hues in the kitchen. They help create focal points and are secondary to the room's most prominent color. In many cases, the room's larger surfaces—the walls, floors, and cabinetry—feature the room's main color while other elements like the furniture, rugs, and accessories are used to interject spots of stronger, more spirited shades. In design, there is an old rule of thumb that states for a hue to become an effective accent color, it must be repeated at least five times in the room. In some kitchens, the chosen shade may be fixed to elements like tile and cabinetry, making it a somewhat permanent player in the room. On the other hand, it can tint napkins, vases, cushions, and jars, making it easily removed and replaced, depending on the season or simple whim of the homeowner.

The robustly colored kitchen at the left is a wonderful example of how accent colors can impact a space with a distinctive, unified look. Here, both blue and red are accents to the room's most prominent weathered-green color. As part of the striking tile backsplash, blue is repeated in the striped draperies and stool cushions, the silver-topped canisters, and boldly painted Mexican ceramics placed about. Red is similarly dispersed in the kitchen. Both colors significantly contribute to the overall feel of the space by adding dimension and points of interest throughout the room.

PERFORMANCE

What room has more talent than the kitchen? In some homes it performs solely as the center for food preparation. However, more frequently it plays an assortment of other parts including that of the dining room, home office, family room, laundry room and social center of the house. To successfully play these many roles, the kitchen's "wardrobe" is very important. The room must be properly attired to perform and entertain in its many portrayals. This is where detail comes into play. It completes the "costume" of the room. With the functional roles of the kitchen in mind, detail can be used to combine the traditionally disjoined rooms into one beautiful and efficient space. It blurs the customary boundaries of the separate areas, smoothly integrating their assorted practical and decorative elements . . . computers to sofas, desks to washing machines, dining tables to utility nooks. The result is an evolved room—a distinctively designed kitchen created to serve the divers purposes and activities unique to the individual homeowner.

What role do you ask your kitchen to play? Is it purely for cooking or is it, instead, the social center in which neighbors and family meet for chitchat and meals throughout the day? It may even be a richly fashioned living area—home to everyday activities as well as special entertaining. Determining the performing role of your kitchen is the key to creating an efficient and uniquely personalized space. This decision reflects the way you plan to spend time in the room and, as a result, affects nearly every design decision from its functional layout to the seemingly endless details used throughout. The trick is to incorporate detail not only that facilitates the activities you intend for this space, but also brings a taste of your personal style to the room.

Like a "tight ship" describes not only the efficiency of a cook-in kitchen, but in many cases, its spatial restrictions as well. Here, the kitchen is strictly defined as a room in which to cook. Any activities outside of preparing food are assigned to other areas of the home. Although the cook-in kitchen has a singular purpose and limited space, it does not mean it has limited style. Character is brought to this room through the forms and finishes of its surfaces and essential objects. Superfluous items are banished, as there is little room for more than the functional components of the working kitchen.

From the room's walls and appliances to the everyday drawer pulls, utensils, and cookware, detail is added to the cook-in kitchen. A stainless-steel ladle replaces a large plastic spoon. A sparkling cabinet door relieves a flat laminated one. In this

COOK-IN

constrained room, even the smallest of changes can have a big impact on its appearance. A careful eye considers every possibility and exploits the opportunity to bring a personalized look by stylizing even the simplest of the room's parts and pieces. This is how a cook-in kitchen really "gets cooking."

To make the most of what is oftentimes the limited space of the cook-in kitchen requires imagination, discipline, and an attention to detail. Foremost, a critical eye eliminates cluttering excess in everything from dishes to utensils, appliances to fixtures. It is wise to determine what is necessary and keep the best of these. Discard the remaining items as they use valuable space in this already tight room. For storage, fitted cabinets with floor-to-ceiling shelves, pullout work surfaces, and hidden storage features work best in the cramped cook-in kitchen. Plate racks, stacked baskets, hanging butcher racks, wall shelves, and under-counter cup hooks also help with storage while taking advantage of unused space and adding character to the kitchen.

Be careful not to let these storage fixtures overwhelm the room as it is best aesthetically to keep the area open, bright, and uncomplicated. Unobstructed windows and natural light help as they visually expand the space. So do soft neutral colors, reflective finishes, glass, and plain or large-patterned surfaces. To heighten the room, vertical stripes, tall cabinets, a white ceiling, uplights, and ceiling molding can help dramatically. Finally, the finishing touches that make the space uniquely personal are achieved through the careful selection and display of the room's essentials. The colors, shapes, and arrangement of everyday dishes become this room's art. So do patterned dish towels, spice-filled canisters, eye-catching drawer pulls, and hanging chrome cooking utensils. The character of these necessities replaces that of idle knickknacks and accessories used to bring unique personality to less spatially challenged rooms in the home.

PAGE 118
In a modern kitchen, it is the details that provide intrigue and excitement for the space. The clean fitted look of this small area features an ungrouted terrazzo backsplash, honey maple cabinetry, glossy blue laminates, and a breakfast bar imaginatively topped with a piece of sandblasted glass framed in stainless steel.

OPPOSITE BOTTOM LEFT
This tight kitchen derives its personality from bold colors and quirky accessories. Every surface is designed to function efficiently, yet is also detailed to bring strong character to the room. Storage shelves with open display, bright tile countertops, and unadorned walls painted in multiple hues, all contribute to the room's decorative impact.

OPPOSITE UPPER RIGHT
When space is tight, imaginative display of everyday items is used to create interest. Here, textured-glass door fronts and under-counter utensils show off the constantly used tools of the room. Clear white surfaces help expand this room visually.

LEFT
The simple contrast of bold textures, finishes, and shapes can bring theatre to a small kitchen. Like sculpture, this kitchen's custom stove hood and base are shaped from brushed stainless steel. The rich textures and colors of the rajah-slate floor, deep-toned mahogany, and shiny black granite complete the dramatic effect. A collection of functional utensils becomes the room's art.

121

The concept of a kitchen that doubles as a dining room is hardly new. In centuries past, food was cooked in a wood-burning hearth that was just feet away from the home's dining table. The main difference between the dine-in kitchen of then and now is that today's version is created by choice. Many people have opted for a combination kitchen/dining room, preferring the convenience, efficiency, and casual atmosphere it offers. This decision either does away with the rarely used formal dining room or adds to it another location for friends and family to gather and eat. In fact, with the options of the breakfast bar, the pull-up center island, the casual dining nook, as well as the main dining area, your plate of food could get cold as you wander around just trying to decide on the area in

DINE-IN

which you want to dine. The decorative challenge that accompanies the dine-in kitchen lies in creating a space that accommodates the task-oriented nature of the kitchen while offering a comfortable, pleasing, and sometimes elegant environment for the dining experience. This is a job for detail. It gives your dine-in kitchen a personalized style, while promoting the room's successful changing of roles from a hardworking cooking space to a welcoming, "I could just sit here for hours," dining area.

Creating a space that effectively pairs the cooking atmosphere of a working kitchen with the ambience of a relaxing dining room is a challenge. Detail helps accomplish this. The cooking and dining areas should be distinct from each other, and yet they must be connected decoratively to give the room a sense of continuity and harmony. There are many ways to accomplish this. If, for instance, the two "zones" feature different flooring treatments or color stories, a common treatment or texture of the walls can visually marry the two areas together. So, too, can an unusual uniform ceiling treatment or even cabinetry that flows from one area into the other. On the other hand, if the two areas appear too similar, distinct details should be used in one area and not in the other. Floor rugs, distinctive light fixtures, or dissimilar surface treatments can help differentiate the cooking and eating areas while still allowing for a sense of continuity. Even the simple use of a few minor details—a common hardware, accent color, or fabric can be used in both parts of the dine-in kitchen to give it a sense of unity and cohesion. The result is a beautifully styled room that effortlessly combines the two areas with common detail.

LEFT
A diagonally set stone floor, honey-colored woodwork, and richly finished walls unite this kitchen with the adjoining dining area. A series of arches supported by stone columns encloses the dining area so that it can also be enjoyed separately from the working kitchen.

RIGHT
A subtle composition of warm woods, rich fabrics, and soft colors effectively marries the cooking and dining areas of this open kitchen. At the same time, to define the separate areas, a circular "stage" is created for the dining table with tile flooring, a bi-level ceiling, and a dimmable hanging light.

PAGE 123
A massive harvest table sets the tone and style for this inviting kitchen. Attention to color, texture, and scale makes the remaining decorative elements of the room—paneled cabinetry, stone floors, and bordered plaster walls—the perfect complements to the prized table.

Used for more than the day's first meal, the breakfast bar has become one of the most popular fixtures in today's kitchen. There is rarely a time when someone isn't perched here on a stool eating, working, or just keeping the cook company. In smaller kitchens, the breakfast bar often replaces a formal dining area that requires more space; while in other kitchens, it structurally divides open floor plans, separating the cooking area from a more formal dining or living area. Uniquely detailed, it can be dressed in elegant granite and polished woods, or stylishly garbed in stainless steel, tile, or glass. It can be free-formed with soft curves or defined with strong lines and corners. It can be table or counter height and feature open display niches, storage shelves, and even convenient sinks adding to its functional talents. And the seating, . . . well, the options are limitless. From chairs to stools, they surround the breakfast bar like stylish party-goers gathering in celebration.

ABOVE
Elevated above the L-shaped island, this granite-topped breakfast bar mirrors the high-tech style of the room. In shape, it mimics the free-form shelves above the stainless-steel cabinetry. Its three stools are works of art themselves and provide the perfect vantage point from which to enjoy the lavish, furturistic detail throughout the room.

LEFT
Rule number one: there are no rules. This kitchen combines the convenience of an island-attached breakfast bar with the unusual scale and height of a traditional kitchen table. The advantages of both are achieved—the ease of oven to table serving with the ability to seat many more than the common breakfast bar can accommodate.

OPPOSITE
A lover of the breakfast bar, this smartly styled kitchen features two versions of this popular sitting station. The three-stool bar is equipped with the kitchen sink, and provides a more casual place to eat, visit with the chef, and help with the meal's preparation. On the other hand, the L-shaped counter is higher and is equipped with more luxurious barstools for those on-lookers who like to linger but not participate in the room's work.

Is today's kitchen a cooking room in which we live or a living room in which we cook? In many cases it is both. Open floor plans and integrated seating and conversation areas have resulted in expanded kitchens that have literally replaced the traditional stand-alone living room. Unlike the off-limits living room of yesterday, the live-in kitchen is a room shared with, rather than flaunted to, the friends and

LIVE-IN

family we invite into the heart of the home. It offers comfort and ease while annexing the practical nature of the food-oriented space. It is a place to gather not only during a meal, but also before and after. Everyone becomes a participant, or at least an audience member, of the culinary adventures taking place around the stove. At the same time, the chef can share in the conversations and activities taking place in the living area while still being at arm's reach of the boiling pots. For families, this layout offers an un-obstructive view that allows supervision of children at play while, at the same time, preparing the daily meals. It is truly a multifunctional space. In fact, when combined with a dining area, the live-in kitchen performs all the household functions short of the sleeping and bathing. It un-questionably sets the stage for the quality of life enjoyed in the home. For this reason, the importance of its detail cannot be overstated. It harmoniously connects the purpose-oriented zones of the room, while reflecting the style and interests of those whose lives are lived in the space.

LEFT
Sometimes a detail is most intriguing when it is used where it would be least expected. In this kitchen, the surfaces, lighting fixtures, and accessories are more at home in a modern art exhibit than in a working kitchen. The result is a high-energy space that is held together by common colors, free-form designs, and unique provocative forms in furnishings and fixtures.

ABOVE
Reflecting an eclectic take on loft-living, this kitchen opens up to a great room accented with Roman columns, Spanish furnishings, and contemporary angled architecture. With the exception of its stained-glass window, the kitchen is devoid of bold detail that would compete with the strong statements of style found throughout the open area.

UPPER RIGHT
Color is the most immediate of this room's characteristics unifying the kitchen's open living areas. From cobalt to cerulean, blue brings a cool relaxed feel to this home.

RIGHT
Patterned wooden floors, plaid accent pillows, and linear grids on windows and cabinetry give this open room a coordinated and comfortable feel.

As the live-in kitchen has become the home's "great room," its design and detail have evolved with the many roles it plays. The large and open area incorporates decorative elements once thought to be out-of-bounds to the cooking quarter of the home. Elegant fabrics, polished marble, distinctive light fixtures, and fine woods are now common to this room. So are ornately framed art, refined collectibles, and exquisite rugs. Cabinetry is the room's furniture with carvings and finishes as beautifully executed as those of fine pieces proudly placed in the formal living room of yesterday.

The richly appointed live-in kitchen shares its personality with neighboring rooms as its decorative detail flows into the entry and main halls of the home, as well as the nearby den, study, and even outdoor areas. This continuity of character, color, and texture wonderfully blends the kitchen with the rest of the home, allowing one to move from room to room without experiencing an interruption in the style and personality that makes the space unique and beautiful.

RIGHT
Vast open rooms often create a discomforting "lost" feeling. To avoid this effect, this spectacularly detailed home calls on every surface to both define and personalize the gathering areas throughout the voluminous kitchen-dining-living room. Like hovering clouds, the free-formed levels on the ceiling direct the eye and help define the spaces beneath them. Granite-topped islands and countertops at various levels also divide the room into separate sitting and working areas. Task specific, some of these areas are for preparing and cooking foods, while others are designed for serving and entertaining. A neutral stone floor throughout keeps the area from being too chopped up, while rugged stacked-stone walls and broad open windows give texture and light to the impressive space.

The kitchen is a hub of activity and clearly, cooking is just the beginning of the tasks that take place here. Because of the kitchen's many jobs, specially designed work areas and neighboring rooms are developed to accommodate the endless demands on this vital space. The kitchen is like a crew boss handing out duties to its helpers—the laundry room, corner desk, pantry, and hobby areas, all line up for work. So, too, do special

OFF THE KITCHEN

interest areas including wine cellars, conservatories, and garden rooms. Even the neighboring patio helps with the cooking, dining, and entertaining assignments

imposed on the kitchen. Each of these areas have the same potential for stunning style as does the kitchen. The same attention to detail that brings the kitchen to life should be shared with its "assistants," giving them a character as vibrant and distinctive as that of their leader.

Why should the many service and work areas of the home not share in the same decorative detail that is lavished on the kitchen. After all, the daily activities conducted in these spaces can become more enjoyable if their design receives the same attention as that given to the home's cooking center. Distinctive flooring can flow from the kitchen as can color infused walls, distinctive hardware, unique accessories, and imaginative surface treatments. These rooms clearly provide opportunity to incorporate imaginative details that bring a home to life, even in its most remote corners.

PAGE 135
While built-in wine racks are a popular feature in many of today's kitchens, a full-scale wine cellar is a luxury enjoyed by few. This awe-inspiring room leaves no surface untouched. Everywhere you look, from the battered studded door, to the torch wall sconce, stone banister and antique "tasting chair," this room's details create an atmosphere that lives up to the fine wines it houses.

OPPOSITE UPPER LEFT
Oftentimes the poor cousin to the well-decorated kitchen, the laundry room can be given new life with the simplest of details. In this room, cabinetry and flooring continue from the neighboring kitchen, while handsome hardware, stone backsplashes, and a ceiling rack adorned with dried flowers and woven baskets give the room its own unique personality.

OPPOSITE LOWER LEFT
This desk is beautifully incorporated into a fresh classic kitchen. It is perfectly placed beneath a window with good light and a great view. Multiple drawers and overhead shelves equip the work space with ample storage and display space.

OPPOSITE LOWER RIGHT
An alternative to the home's full-service kitchen, this mini-kitchen and laundry is located right off the master bedroom. Clean and spare in surface and fixture detail, this area relies on warm wood, treated glass, and structured hardware to define its personality and straightforward purpose.

UPPER LEFT
This multipurpose space shares in the kitchen's warm character and comforting detail. Honey-toned cabinets lead from the kitchen to glass-front hutches displaying cherished dinnerware and china. A casual dining nook is upholstered with fabrics that also are featured in the main cooking area. A bulletin board, cookbooks, and a small TV make this a wonderful personalized space to take momentary refuge from the more demanding room next door.

LOWER LEFT
The mudroom is oftentimes a bland transition space from the outdoors into the kitchen. Why not bring it to life with your own unique passions? Here, an avid gardener developed a potting room that is home to all the tools of the trade. Handsome cabinetry and a stainless-steel set-in-stone sink are the workhorses of the space. Customized upper display cabinets, bin-pull hardware, and rough-hewn walls are just a few of the elements that bring a desired sense of nature into the home.

Tempted by the irresistible pleasures of dining and living outdoors, today's kitchen is oftentimes drawn outside onto beautifully designed patios, porches, and decks. These areas are an extension of the indoor kitchen and commonly share many of its practical and decorative elements. In climates where year-round enjoyment of the patio is possible, a full range of appliances can be designed into an outdoor space, turning it into a fully functioning kitchen. The location and placement of this area should be protected from the elements and placed close to the interior kitchen, giving easy access to it. In areas where winter curtails outdoor dining, portable appliances and grills can be integrated into outdoor cooking areas, then be removed during the off-season. In both cases, the range of outdoor appliances available has never been greater for the enthusiast of al fresco dining.

These outdoor sanctuaries can be as beautifully and comfortably appointed as the interior kitchen and living areas. Materials once considered appropriate for only indoor use have found their way onto the patio and porch. Exotic rattan, rich handcarved woods, intricately woven wicker, and even upholstery have joined beautifully scrolled iron and solid teak outdoors. In fact, special finishes, synthetic materials, and protective fabric treatments have made the use of many traditionally "indoor" materials common and practical in the outdoor kitchen. Further extending the personality of the indoor kitchen, stone and tile flooring can flow from the inside to the outside. So can decorative wall finishes, unique cabinetry, and oftentimes special lighting fixtures. Distinct accent colors as well as patterned fabrics and accessories also can be used to successfully link both areas.

LEFT
This patio integrates all the working components of its indoor counterpart to create a fully functioning outdoor kitchen. Across from the enclosure housing the cabinetry, sink, and refrigerator is a beam-covered cooking area that overlooks the eating counter and pool beyond.

OPPOSITE
Outdoor kitchens come in all shapes and sizes. This festive setting incorporates a sink, appliances, and inviting banco seating into the curved wall of this irresistible outdoor living area.

Brad Mee is a writer and author, who specializes in interiors and homes. His background in design includes work in the fields of interior and fashion design, as well as advertising and home furnishings. This book is the follow-up title to Mee's *Design Is in the Details*, which was published in 2001. Brad resides in Phoenix, Arizona.

From the Author:

I would like to express my appreciation to the many people who made this project possible.

This book could not exist without the outstanding work of the many creative designers, architects, builders, manufacturers and artisans featured within. Your projects are an inspiration and I thank you for your contributions. To the talented photographers who captured the magic of these rooms and homes, thank you. It is the genius of your images that brings the pages of this book to life. My gratitude also goes to the gracious homeowners who shared their homes and opened the doors to their wonderful kitchens.

My thanks go to *Phoenix Home & Garden Magazine* as many of the images shown in this book originally appeared in this beautiful publication. The efforts and talents of Ph&G editor, Linda J. Barkman, and art director, Margie Van Zee, are greatly appreciated. Additional thanks go to *Utah Style and Design Magazine* and editor, Andrea Malouf, for their contributions to this project.

Finally, I am especially grateful to my friends at Chapelle, Ltd., and to my editor, Karmen Quinney. Your support, suggestions, and friendship proved invaluable. For his substantial contributions and dedication to this project, I thank Dino Tonn. Dino, once again your photography bears witness to your remarkable talent.

Dino Tonn Photography
5433 East Kathleen Road
Phoenix, Arizona 85254
(602) 765-0455
An attention to detail and true artistry in lighting have made Dino Tonn one of the leading architectural photographers in the Southwest. Specializing in award-winning architectural and golf course photography, Tonn has been photographing much of the Southwest's finest architecture for the past 12 years. He serves clients in the hospitality field as well as architects, interior designers, developers, and many other design-related businesses and publications. His work has been featured in regional and national publications. Tonn is a native of Arizona and resides in Scottsdale, Arizona, with his wife and two children.

Lydia Cutter
1029 North George Mason Drive
Arlington, Virginia 22205
(703) 741-0424
A specialist in interior photography, Lydia Cutter serves residential and commercial clients nationwide. In addition to her photography, she also produces fine art that adorns beautiful homes as well as commercial buildings throughout the country. Her photographic work has been featured in national and regional interior publications. Cutter resides in Arlington, Virginia.

Scot Zimmerman
P.O. Box 289
261 North 400 West
Heber City, Utah 84032–0289
(800) 654-7897 / zimfolks@sprynet.com
Scot Zimmerman is an architectural photographer. During the last twenty years, his accomplishments include: photographing and authoring six books, having his photographs featured in over 45 books, regularly contributing to national and regional architectural and home & garden publications, and completing ongoing professional assignments across the country. Zimmerman's work has been exhibited in six museums.

Bill Timmerman
382 North First Avenue
Phoenix, Arizona 85003
(602) 420-9325
A professional photographer for 24 years, Bill Timmerman's primary focus became architectural photography after his images of the Phoenix Central Library (architect Will Bruder) were published internationally. His ever expanding clientele includes accomplished contemporary architects and interior designers. He has been a resident of Phoenix, Arizona, for 16 years.

David Michael Miller Associates
7034 East First Avenue
Scottsdale, Arizona 85251
(480) 425-7545
A custom interior design studio, committed to creating unique and beautiful environments for its clients.

Ann Sacks
(800) 278-8453 / www.annsacks.com
From the well-worn beauty of centuries-old marble to the whimsical spirit of one-of-a-kind art tiles, inspirational designs have made Ann Sacks number one in fine tile and stone products. That leadership now extends to luxury plumbing products that are both thrilling and unexpected.

SieMatic
(800) 765-5266 / www.siematic.com
Behind the doors of SieMatic custom cabinetry stands a world filled with simple form, elegant design, and custom options—a place rich in tradition and alive with imagination and innovation. The SieMatic line includes over 81 door styles and 90 standard finishes for use throughout the home.

Wood-Mode
(800) 635-7500 / www.wood-mode.com
With 60 years of experience, Wood-Mode is America's premier manufacturer of custom built-in cabinetry for every room in the home. Backed by a Lifetime Limited Warranty, the line features more than 75 door styles and 100 finishes in framed and frameless construction, as well as a wide selection of interior convenience options to maximize storage possibilities.

ACKNOWLEDGMENTS

PHOTOGRAPHY

Lydia Cutter 2, 23, 55, 87, 110

Bill Timmerman 14–15, 27, 29, 78(ul), 89(ur)(ctr)(lr), 100(l), 107(ll)

Dino Tonn 1, 4–5, 6(l)(r), 7(l)(ctr)(r), 9, 11, 18–21, 22(ul)(ur)(lr), 24–25, 30–34, 35(ul)(ctr)(ll), 36–37, 39(ll), 40, 41(ur), 43, 45, 46(ur), 47(ll)(ur), 48–49, 51, 52(ul)(ur), 53, 58–60, 62–63, 65(r), 67(l), 69, 72(ul)(lr), 73–74, 75(ll)(ur), 76–77, 81(ul)(ll), 82–85, 86(l)(lr), 88, 90, 93–94, 95(ul)(ll), 98–99, 101(r), 104(ul)(ctr)(lr), 105(l), 107(ur), 108(l), 113(ur), 114–115, 117–119, 120(ll), 121(l), 122–125, 126(ll), (ur), 127, 130, 131(ur)(lr), 132–135, 136(ul)(lr), 139

Margie Van Zee (photostylist) 6(l), 7(ctr), 9, 11, 19, 22(ur), 32–33, 35(ul), 40, 46(ur), 48–49, 51, 52(ul), 53, 58(l), 59(r), 60, 65(r), 72(lr)(ul), 73, 75(ll)(ur), 81(lr)(ul), 84–85, 86(lr)(l), 90, 93, 95(ur), 100(r), 105(l), 118, 120(ll), 126(ur), 134, 136(lr), 139

Scot Zimmerman 17(lr), 38, 70–71, 112(ur), 138

INTERIOR DESIGN

American Classic Kitchens 46(lr)

Andel Interiors, Fountain Hills, AZ
    Martha Andreghetti 130

Barnes, R. Kent 64(l)

Bess Jones Interiors, Scottsdale, AZ 35(ll), 76–77, 81(ul), 93, 104(ctr), 134

Billi Springer & Associates, Scottsdale, AZ 6(l), 11, 51, 95(ul)

Bowden & Quinn Interior Design, Scottsdale, AZ
    Kathleen Villella 123

Bron Design Group Interiors, Phoenix, AZ
    Eric and Dorothy Bron 60

Carol Buto Designs, Scottsdale, AZ 58(l), 75(ur), 124

Casa del Encanto, Scottsdale, AZ
    Luis Corona and Michael Barron 139

David Michael Miller Associates Interior Design, Scottsdale, AZ
    14–15, 27, 29, 78(ul), 88, 89(ur)(ctr)(lr), 94(r), 100(l), 107(ll)

Debi Weber Interior Design, Scottsdale, AZ 32

Desert Cove Interiors, Phoenix, AZ
    Sonja Parsons 20–21, 62–63

Dianne Carol Interiors, Scottsdale, AZ 30–31

Do Daz Design Firm, Scottsdale, AZ
    Terri Mulmed NCIDQ, ASID 36–37, 136(ul)

Elements of Design, Scottsdale, AZ
    Jo Ann Johnston 23

Emerald Designs, Sunriver, OR
    Vicki Banta 1(l)(ctr)(r)

est. est. Interior Design, Scottsdale, AZ
    Tom Turner 48–49, 136(lr)
    Tony Sutton 108(l)

European Design Custom Cabinetry
    Alan Rosenthal 113

Evans, Sandra 52(ul), 53

Friedman & Shields Interior Design, Scottsdale, AZ
    Jan Friedman and Traci Shields 126(ur)

Graber Designs, Ltd., Scottsdale, AZ
    Marsha Graber 46(ur)

Inter Plan Design Group, Scottsdale, AZ
    Larry Lake 47(ll), 82–83, 98–99

Interior Designations, Scottsdale, AZ
    Marsha Amato 105(l)

Interior Studio Group, Scottsdale, AZ
    Carol Minchew 86(l)(lr)

Jamie Herzlinger Interiors, Scottsdale, AZ 22(ul)(lr), 24–25

Kitchell Interior Design Associates, Scottsdale, AZ
    Nancy Kitchell 107(ur)

Knoell Quidort Architects, Phoenix, AZ
    Sandra Evans 52(ul), 53

Lisa Wagenhals Interior Design, Scottsdale, AZ 9

Long, Kay 104(ll), 144

McGowen, Peggy CKD, CBD, ASID 80

Mee, Brad 35(ctr)

Michael Glassman Design, Sacramento, CA 138

North Peak Design, Scottsdale, AZ
    Donna Haugen 132–133

Ostrom, Barbara ASID 54(ll), 57, 78(ll)

Paula Berg Design Associates, Scottsdale, AZ 2, 55, 87

Paula den Boer Interior Design, Scottsdale, AZ 7(l), 69, 135

Pembrook Lane Interiors, Phoenix, AZ
    Brenda Heuring Harris 104(ul)

Saunder, Eddie 50, 61

Schick Design Group, Scottsdale, AZ
    Jonelle K. Schick 121

Smith & Dana Associates, Scottsdale, AZ
    Carol Smith 33, 35(ul), 75(ll)

St. John, Jenessa, Scottsdale, AZ 104(lr)

Stevan's Furniture, Phoenix, AZ
    Stevan Thompson and Bernadean Fuller 18–19

Tamasy, Linda 101(ll)

Teresa DeLellis Design Associates, Carefree, AZ 114–115

Thurnauer, Eileen 113(ll)

Wales, Kelly and Shari (owners) 70–71

William Hargrave Interior Designer, Flagstaff, AZ 7(ctr), 22(ur), 90

Wiseman & Gale Interiors, Scottsdale, AZ
    Anne Gale 84–85
    Donna Vallone and Anne Gale 52(ll)
    Jana Parker Lee 65(r), 95(ll)
    Sue Calvin 101

Wolf, Matt 54(ur)

KITCHEN DESIGN

Atelier, Inc., Scottsdale, AZ
    Steve Johnson 126(ur)

Duncan Fuller Interiors, Birmingham, MI
    Ann Armstrong Heath 81(ll)

Fortner, Bruce 120(ll)

Evans, Sandra and owner 52(ul), 53

Hiline Design, Ltd., Scottsdale, AZ
    Rob Rubin 118–119

Mary Fisher Kitchen and Bath Design 6(l), 11
Trent Gasbarra Interior Designer 59(ll)

ARCHITECTS

Abramson Architects, Culver City, CA 27, 29, 89(ur)
Alan Tafoya Architect, Carefree, AZ 6(l), 11, 51, 84–85, 95(ul)
Bokal & Sneed Architects, Del Mar, CA 14–15, 78(ul), 89(ctr)(lr)
Concepts GDL Architects, Scottsdale, AZ
    Gerald Lamb 58(l)
Conk Architects, Scottsdale, AZ
    Joe Conk 58(l)
David Dodge Architect, Taliesin, AZ 38
Frances Walker Architect, Scottsdale, AZ 20–21
Fulton Architects, Scottsdale, AZ
    George Fulton 93
George Christiansen Architect, Phoenix, AZ 52(ll)
Gordon Rogers Architect, Inc., AIA, Phoenix, AZ 58(ctr)
H&S International Architects, Scottsdale, AZ 88
    Bing Hu 40, 75(ur), 124
Kottke Architecture
    James Kottke AIA 104(lr)
Lash McDaniel Architect, Scottsdale, AZ 101, 108(l)
Michael Johnson Architect, Cave Creek, AZ 112(ur)
Miller Associates Old World Building Design, Scottsdale, AZ
    Clint Miller 7(r), 117
Rick Daugherty Architect, Scottsdale, AZ 86(l)(lr)
RJ Bacon & Co., Phoenix, AZ
    Bob Bacon 48–49, 60, 136(lr)
Urban Design Associates, Scottsdale, AZ
    Lee Hutchison 1, 7(l), 69, 76–77, 81(ul), 134–135

BUILDERS

Alexander Development Corp., Scottsdale, AZ
    Ken Alexander 107(ur)
Anthony Wilder Design/Build, Inc. 110
Arnette-Romero Builders, Scottsdale, AZ 6(l), 11, 84–85
Calvis Wyatt Luxury Homes 74
Camelot Homes, Scottsdale, AZ 47(ur), 131(lr)
Classic Stellar Homes, Phoenix, AZ 47(ll), 82–83, 98–99
Custom Homes by Randy Cozens, Scottsdale, AZ 59(r)
Dave Hansen Construction, Inc., Scottsdale, AZ 32
Gietz Master Builders, Scottsdale, AZ
    Gary Gietz 104(lr), 139
Kitchell Custom Homes, Phoenix, AZ 60, 86(l)(lr), 108(l)
Lithicum Construction, Scottsdale, AZ 40
Madison Couturier Custom Homes, Scottsdale, AZ
    Dan Couturier 51, 95(ul)
Monterey Homes, Scottsdale, AZ 125(r)
RA Merritt Custom Homes, Scottsdale, AZ 88
R.J. Gurley Construction, Scottsdale, AZ 48–49, 136(lr)

Rowland Luxury Homes, Phoenix, AZ 81(ul), 134
Sandella Custom Builders, Fountain Hills, AZ 130
Salcito Custom Homes, Scottsdale, AZ 6(r), 35(ll), 43, 58(ctr), 93, 104(ctr), 136(ul)
Shiloh Custom Homes, Scottsdale, AZ 1, 7(l), 69, 76–77, 135
Sivage Thomas Homes 126(ll)
Tuscan Estate Homes, Scottsdale, AZ 75(ur), 124

CABINETRY

All Wood Treasures (kitchen island) 114–115
Architectural Wood Interiors Cabinetry, Phoenix, AZ
    Pierre Langue 65(r), 95(ll)
Arizona Custom Cabinets, Peoria, AZ 35(ll), 93, 104(ctr)
Copperstate Cabinet Company, Phoenix, AZ 132–133
Desert Cove Woodworks, Phoenix, AZ
    Matt Parsons 20–21, 62–63
European Design Custom Cabinetry, Scottsdale, AZ
    Alan Rosenthal 39(ll), 41(ur), 48–49, 113(ur), 127, 136(lr)
Hiline Design, Ltd., Scottsdale, AZ 52(ul), 53, 88
Inspirations, Palm Desert, CA
    Beth Pachachi 6(r), 40, 43
Jordan & Jordan, Scottsdale, AZ 120(ll)
Kiesler Enterprises, Phoenix, AZ
    Gary Kiesler 1, 7(l), 69, 81(ll)(ul), 134–135
Rysso-Peters, Inc., Phoenix, AZ 67, 123
SieMatic Cabinetry 17(ll), 26, 28(lr), 35(ur), 41(ul)(ctr)(lr), 65(ll), 112(ll), 118–119, 128–129, 140
Snaidero, Scottsdale, AZ 107(ur)
Valley Woodworks, Fountain Hills, AZ 6(l), 11
Wood-Mode Cabinetry 13, 16, 17(ul), 28(ul)(ur)(ll), 46(lr), 47(lr), 50, 54(ur)(ll), 57, 61, 64(l)(lr), 75(lr), 78(ll), 80, 96–97, 101(ll), 104(ur), 109, 113(ll), 120(ur), 136(ll), 137(ul)(ll)

PRODUCTS

Ann Sacks 39(ur), 41(ll), 78(ur), 79(r), 81(lr)
Audio Visions, Lake Forest, CA
    Paul Self 108(l)
Ceramica, Scottsdale, AZ (tile) 9
Heartland Kitchen Appliances, Ontario, Canada 72(ul)(lr)
Progressive Concrete Works, Phoenix, AZ (floors) 45, 101
Stockett Tile & Granite, Scottsdale, AZ 7(l), 18–19, 48–49, 69, 81(ul), 88, 134–135, 136(lr)
Voita, Stephen (artwork) 107(ur)

PHOTODISKS

Artiville, LLC Images (© 1997) 131(ul)
Corbis Corporation Images (© 1999, 2000) 35(lr), 78(lr)
Photodisc, Inc. Images (© 1999, 2000, 2001) 17(ctr), 22(ctr), 28(ctr), 91, 103

Every effort has been made to credit all contributors. We apologize in advance for any unintentional omission and would be pleased to insert the appropriate acknowledgment in any subsequent edition.

INDEX

accent colors 115, 138

Accessories 92–97

Acknowledgments 141

Appliances 27, 50, 52, 68, 70–75, 89, 138

Artistic Ingredients 41

Artistic Style 36–41

backsplash(s) . . . 27, 39, 52, 54, 61, 85, 94, 115, 137

banco seating 138

Basic Ingredients 68–89

breakfast bar 79, 121–122, 126

butcher block 17, 62, 79

Cabinets 62–67

ceiling 56, 61, 114

chandelier(s) 20, 30, 56, 84–85, 105, 125

Churchill, Winston 33, 113

Color 110–115

Comforting Ingredients 17

Comforting Style 12–17

Cook-in 118–121

copper 14, 17, 20, 22, 33, 75, 95, 103, 105

Countertops 76–81

country design(s) 12, 67

Credits 142–143

dimmers 86

Dine-in 122–127

Disciplined Ingredients 28

Disciplined Style 24–29

Display(s) . . 50, 64, 98–101, 107

faux finished 18, 22

flagstone 46–47

floor(s) 44, 46

focal point(s) 47, 52, 54, 75, 107, 115

halogen(s) 24, 28, 61, 84, 86, 100

Hanging On 102–107

hanging rack 103, 105

Comfort is a friend's kitchen.
Anonymous

Herbert, George 20

home office 8, 116

Imported Ingredients 35

Imported Style 30–35

Inspired Ingredients 22

Inspired Style 18–23

Introduction 8–9

island(s) 80–81, 108, 122

Le Corbusier 27

lamps 22, 84, 86

laundry room 134, 137

Lighting 82–89

Live-in 128–133

molding 24, 61, 64, 120

Morris, William 97

mosaic(s) 52, 54

mullion doors 64

niches 95, 98, 101, 107

Off the Kitchen 134–139

Overhead 56–61

Performance 116–139

Presentation 42–67

Recipes of Style 10–41

saltillo tile 30, 33

skylights 28, 56, 61, 89

slate 42, 76, 121

Spice 90–115

stencils 52, 56, 61

travertine 48

unfitted cabinets 14, 64–65

Underfoot 44–49

utensils 12, 27, 39, 50, 54, 94–95, 98, 103, 108, 120

vent hood 70, 75

Verticals 50–55

wine cellar(s) 134, 137

Working Accents 108–109